Chri

A few spots
out as a New Yorker

*The History and Stories of the*

# Best Bars of New York

*The History and Stories of the*

# Best Bars of New York

*Jef Klein*

*Nashville, Tennessee • Paducah, Kentucky*

Turner Publishing Company

200 4th Avenue North • Suite 950
Nashville, Tennessee 37219
(615) 255-2665

412 Broadway • P.O. Box 3101
Paducah, Kentucky 42002-3101
(270) 443-0121

www.turnerpublishing.com



Library of Congress Control Number: 2005910413

ISBN: 1-56311-971-4

Printed in the United States of America.

0 9 8 7 6 5 4 3 2

# Contents

# *Acknowledgments*

I love bars for the same reason you do. They are fun to go to, they are even fun to work in. And I say that despite the many brunches I toiled away, slinging quiche under the relentless bleat of Kenny G. on the Muzak. New York City is home to the best bars in the world–the best classy bars, the best neighborhood bars, the best dive bars. New York City wrote the book on bars. I just got to help.

As part of my research, I interviewed people at more than 50 bars. Unfortunately, there wasn't room in the book for them all. But I'd like to say thanks to all the bar owners, managers, bartenders, and regulars I interviewed. They told me some great stories and provided me with archival materials, links to sources, and when I was really lucky, some unforgettable evenings.

There are special thanks due to those of you who made this project even more pleasurable: Jamo McManus (Peter McManus Café), Barbara McGurn (Oak Room), Audrey Saunders (Bemelmans Bar), Joe Diliberto (Cedar Tavern), Gina Ruiz (Chumley's), Bruce Snyder and Diana Biederman ('21' Club), John Ronaghan and Peter O'Connell (Paris Café), Richard McGorty (local historian, Molly's Pub and Shebeen), and Denis Lynch (Milano's).

I'd also like to thank Bill Wander, McSorley's Historian and author, and Dale DeGroff, the undisputed King of Cocktails, for sharing their experiences and insights with me.

Of course I have to thank my mom, Eileen Pimentel. Not only because of all the great stories she told me of New York as it was in the Forties, but because she instilled in me her love for history and research. To my sisters, Gini, Lizzie, Viki, and Jodi, and cousins Cameron and Jackie, thanks for your interest in the book. To my friends who babysat and listened to every story about every bar I visited (and sometimes went along): Peggy Halmi, Rosemary Gohd, Joy Orlan, Cristine Grapa, Laurie Bagley, and Kirk Anderson, thanks again. To my mother-in-law, the late Vera Klein, there is much appreciation, for her help looking after my children, as well as for being a wonderful hostess who taught me so much about hospitality. Thanks are also due to Ron Klein.

But most of all I thank my children, Ellis and Simone. You guys are the bubbles in my champagne.

— Jef Klein, Author

# *Preface*

Part of my job as a publisher is looking for books that need to be created. This is one of those books. I can recount some of the most memorable moments in my life—both good and bad—that happened in some of the settings described in this book. It occurred to me that generations of people have had similar connections to these places, although their experiences and their stories have been more dramatic and historic than my own. With thanks to good friends Taylor and Rawls, we decided that we should investigate, discover and share a collection of these significant stories in a book that describes the remarkable settings where they took place.

This book is not about the liquor or the drinks, although they play a part. It is about the places where life's events have unfolded. It is about the friendships and fights, the business deals and the new ideas, the great conversations and the solitary thinking, that all occurred in these institutions.

When we sat down and tried to determine which establishments to include in *The History and Stories of the Best Bars of New York*, we faced an enormous challenge. Ask any person and they will have an opinion about which ones are "the best." How does one define "the best?" For our part we looked for that indefinable factor that you know when you see it. It is a mixture of longevity, quality and significance. It is the feeling you get when you walk in and know that a lot of things have happened here, important things. While the list can be argued, we welcome the discussion.

We invite people to use this book. To find their place in historical context, to feel a sense of connectedness to the people who share this City and to the people who came before them. For those new to the City or to those who rarely venture outside their neighborhoods, there is an opportunity to explore and to find places they have not yet discovered that offer the comfort and familiarity of their favorite community gathering spaces.

With these thoughts in mind we offer *The History and Stories of the Best Bars of New York.*

— Todd Bottorff, Publisher

*The History and Stories of the*

# Best Bars of New York

CARLOS YACHTS

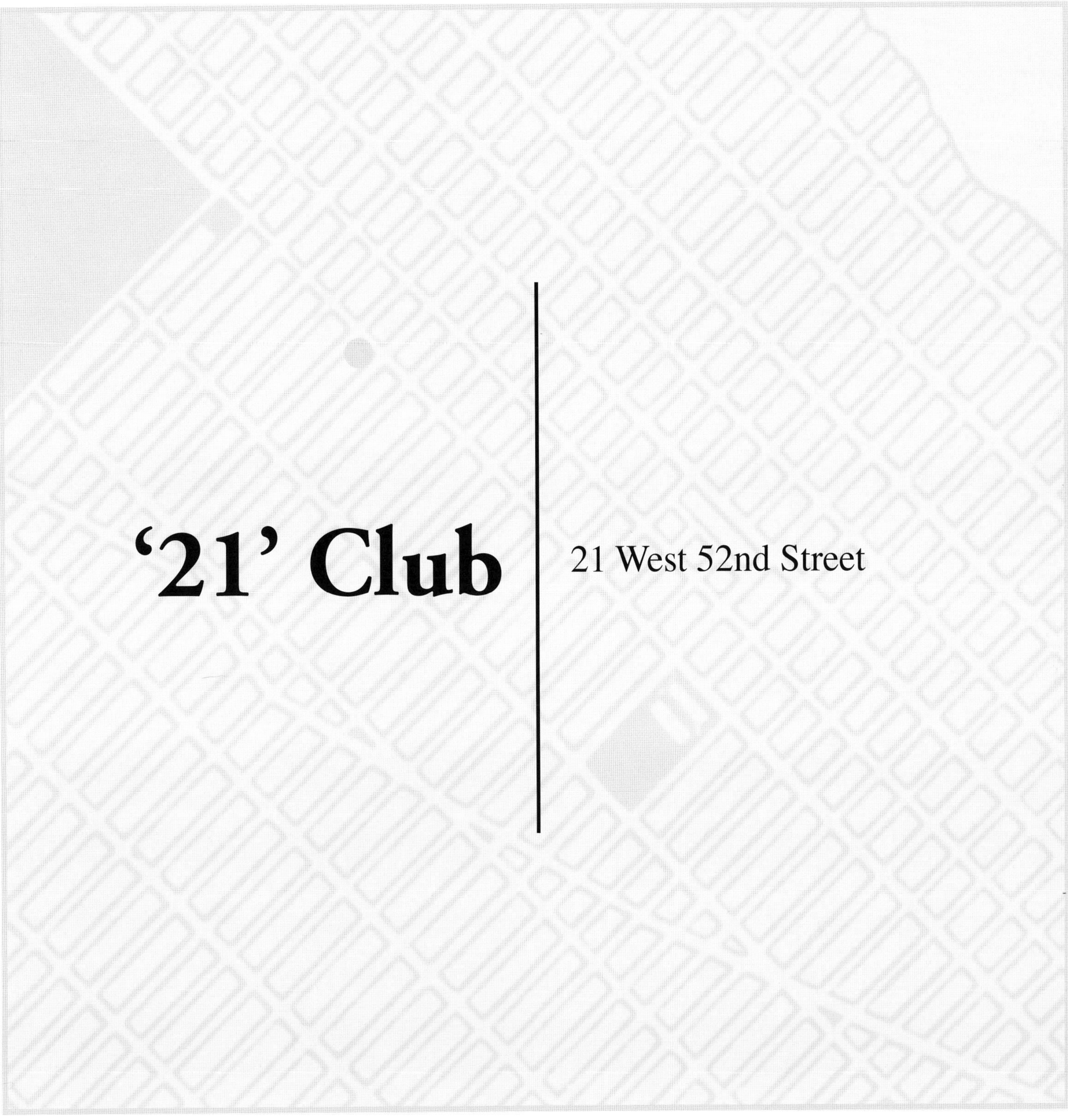

# '21' Club

21 West 52nd Street

OBERT S. LYTLE
SACKATOGA
STABLE
BALLANTINE

*One might think a beginning as a speakeasy would be an inauspicious one. After all, speakeasies were never known for their service, nor for their liquor.*

Your average speakeasy was a dark hideaway where men of dubious integrity served liquor of dubious quality. Down an alley, into a basement, a peephole slides back, and you'd whisper something to gain admittance. Once inside, an ersatz bar made from wood planks and sawhorses. A few tables, a few light bulbs. The place would be packed, though, with every specimen of humankind. The "liquor" was often served in coffee cups, from one of four pitchers; one each for scotch, bourbon, rye, and gin. Often, it was the same brew in each pitcher, but with coloring added to create the effect of different types of liquor. The liquor could be made well, with a real still, such as the artist Neysa McMein had in her apartment. But too often it was stewed up from bottles found lying around the house or worse. Poisonings were not uncommon during Prohibition. Usually there was a drain in the floor for the liquor, and almost always, a back door for a speedy getaway. Such is the quick and dirty portrait of the typical speakeasy, circa New York, 1925.

But this *was* New York, after all, and though it had plenty of homegrown speakeasies in every little neighborhood, it had been home to the best bars in the world. And so, during Prohibition, New York was home to the best speakeasy in the world. And that speakeasy was the '21' Club.

'21' was no ordinary speakeasy. The best liquor and finest wines, the best cuisine, the rarest cigars, and the finest service were offered at this cozy club located in the basement of an elegant townhome just off Fifth Avenue. Best of all, the proprietors kept out the proletariat, making '21' an oasis of fine dining and scintillating conversation in a sea of bathtub gin.

Just gaining admittance to '21' was much more difficult than getting into the average speakeasy. At '21', the clientele were the City's notables—business tycoons, artists, performers, publishers, politicians, and the most interesting personalities from

RADIO

New York and the world. Simply showing up and looking good was not enough to gain admittance. Having money to spend was not enough. This was an exclusive club, always, but exclusive in the best sense of the word: class didn't matter, but having class did. Founded by Jack Kriendler and his cousin, Charlie Berns, the '21' Club started out upscale and hasn't budged a note since.

Even in a city filled with rags-to-riches stories, '21' stands out as a riches-to-riches story. Not that the Kriendlers were rich. The family had modest beginnings on the Lower East Side. Their mother Sadie, a widow, was left to raise eight children. Working as a midwife, and with some help from her brother, Sam Brenner, she got by. Her four sons, Mac, Jack, Pete, and Bob, were determined to get ahead. They enrolled in good colleges and worked nights in their Uncle Sam's bar in the Jewish ghetto on Rivington Street. Uncle Sam cut an elegant figure on the Lower East Side in those days, with his handmade suits, faultless manners, and diamond ring.

*Even in a city filled with rags-to-riches stories, '21' stands out as a riches-to-riches story.*

When Prohibition hit in 1919, speakeasies blossomed seemingly overnight. The most innocuous little basement tea parlor suddenly became a den of illegality. It quickly became evident that there was money to be made in Prohibition if one got in on the ground floor, so to speak. Jack Kriendler, studying at Fordham University, and with the intrepidity only a college student can have, decided to open his own place. He talked Charlie Berns, studying business at New York University, into "going in" with him. They scraped together the money, and what they couldn't scrape, they borrowed from their Uncle Sam, who hocked his diamond ring for the boys. Jack and Charlie figured they'd make enough money to pay for college and get out of the business. That was more than 75 years ago.

They started off running a cup joint called the Red Head in Greenwich Village. A cup joint was a place that served liquor in tea or coffee cups, with refills coming from flasks or pitchers. The liquor went for a dollar an ounce. By this time, brother Pete Kriendler had joined the staff at age 16, keeping teacups filled and hoping one of the boarding-school flappers from uptown would flirt with him. One of the cashiers at the Red Head was future Broadway legend Mark Hellinger, who regarded his job there as the best time of his life. He could keep as much of the 50 cent cover charge as he wanted, and the cash flowed nightly. The liquor came from Sam Brenner's bootleggers and was kept at the Kriendler's apartment, watched over by Sadie herself. When the Red Head ran out of liquor, Mac and Bob would cart it over, using a little red wagon heaped with "groceries."

> *They started off running a cup joint called the Red Head in Greenwich Village. A cup joint was a place that served liquor in tea or coffee cups, with refills coming from flasks or pitchers.*

Of course, the Mob took interest in the thriving business the Kriendler boys were doing at the Red Head. Thugs were dispatched, and the message was relayed that the notorious Hudson Dusters gang, led by none other than Linkey "The Killer" Mitchell, was about to become partners with the Kriendlers. Resisting with the intrepidity that only college students could have, Jack and Charlie fought back. They must've taken the gangsters by surprise, because they won. (That round, anyway.) Next time they ended up in the hospital, with Charlie receiving 12 stitches in his neck. It became apparent that more focus from law enforcement was called for, and the local police force, with some motivation, was happy to comply. And with that, the Red Head had little more worry about the Mob.

After a couple of years, the Red Head closed down and the cousins opened up a new place in the Village called the Fronton, located in a basement at 88 Washington Place. The boys hired Charlie's cousin, Bill Hardey, to work the door. The door had a peephole and a buzzer in case a revenue agent arrived unexpectedly. Cops they didn't worry about; if the police showed up, it was for a little conversation and a cup or two. Bill was also entertainment coordinator, and five piece bands played nightly. It was a classy joint, a precursor to the '21' Club. Patrons included Edna St. Vincent Millay and Hizzoner Mayor Jimmy Walker. The Fronton was where Jack Kriendler honed his skills as host and realized that the carriage trade would have money to spend long after Prohibition was over.

Moving uptown to 49th Street when construction of a subway station razed their building in the Village, Jack and Charlie opened a new speakeasy that was called several different names over the years to fool revenue men. Mostly, though, it was known as the Puncheon. They decided to do the Fronton one better and make sure that the Puncheon served only the best, whether it was wine, liquor, or food. They set themselves apart from other speakeasy owners. They dressed nattily, as their Uncle Sam Brenner had done. They made sure that the door was handled "just so," and a

fellow by the name of Gus Lux would size you up before letting you in. It was not just a case of blue collars out, blue noses in, but a Puncheon patron had to be "well dressed and well behaved."

Whether it was the bar John O'Hara wrote about in his novel *Butterfield 8* is not known, but he did frequent the Puncheon, and so did other writers. Robert Benchley took a liking to the little place and brought his cronies from the nearby Algonquin Hotel, the famous Round Table crew, to see Jack and Charlie's place. The Algonquin didn't serve liquor, so after lunch at the Round Table, they'd hie over to Neysa McMein's apartment for some home-distilled hootch, ending up later at '21.' Alexander Woollcott, Edna Ferber, George S. Kaufman, Franklin P. Adams, Heywood Broun, Ben Hecht, Charles MacArthur, Donald Ogden Stewart and Dorothy Parker became mainstays at the Puncheon. Yale men adopted the place and called it "Ben Quinn's Kitchen," because Ben Quinn, a Yalie, had walked into the Puncheon and realized he was in the cellar of his former family home. According to legend, he exclaimed, "This is my old house! Martinis for everyone!" Being firmly established as the favored watering hole among writers and college men was a great beginning for Jack and Charlie's joint, and the money flowed in like never before.

Of course raids were always in the offing. Such a place, operating so famously and enjoying such a fine reputation, had to be raided. The Feds came, they saw, and they conquered. H. L. Mencken, a regular, was upset and commented in print, "Why raid a place that is serving good liquor and not poisoning anybody?" One of the sore points of the raids was that liquor was out in plain sight. After this, Jack and Charlie learned to keep the liquor hidden in the attic of the house next door. Someone would crawl out on the roof and through the skylight to retrieve the needed bottles when supplies at the Puncheon ran low. Things seemed back in control and were going well until 1929 and the Stock Market Crash.

When your clientele is made up of some of the richest men in the city, the day they stop being the richest men is a problem. Jack and Charlie decided to front their regulars whatever they needed—no easy task considering the overhead at the Puncheon. Credit was extended, bank checks were accepted, and long-term loans were made. Suddenly the Puncheon was operating more like a bar down on the Bowery than the kind of place where customers didn't even look at the check when they paid. The day the Government closed the banks in 1933, Jack and Charlie handed out $50 bills to any of their customers who needed it.

They wisely figured that neither the Depression nor Prohibition could last forever. What they didn't figure on was the fact that neither could the Puncheon.

The wrecking ball had followed Jack and Charlie uptown. The construction of Rockefeller Center caused them to move once more, in 1930. They wanted to stay in the neighborhood, since the cops there were amenable. They found a place at 21 West 52nd Street, where they could own not just the building, but the land underneath, an important asset in a city like New York. And so, on New Year's Eve, the Puncheon closed, but not until after a legendary house-wrecking party. Jack and Charlie handed out crowbars and pickaxes to guests so they could take the place apart. A mounted cop rode through on his horse. As a last hoorah, someone took the iron gate from the front door of the Puncheon, and the next day it was installed at 21 West 52nd Street. It's still there today.

So, '21' started with a silver spoon in its mouth. It already had an excellent reputation. It already had the best food, drink, and customers the city had to offer. The most famous writers, the wealthiest playboys, and the cleverest and most beautiful women, followed Jack and Charlie from the Puncheon to '21.' Mayor Jimmy Walker had a special booth built in the cellar, where the wine and booze were kept, so he could entertain discreetly in case of a raid. Virtually anyone who was *anyone* went to '21.' Jack and Charlie, joined by Kriendler brothers Mac and Pete, had hit the pinnacle of bar ownership in New York. The only place to go from there was…up.

And up they went.

'21' was located in a townhouse on 52nd Street, which was soon to become known as "Swing Street." At that time there were 38 speakeasies on the block of 52nd Street between 5th and 6th Avenues alone. Just across Fifth Avenue, on 53rd near Madison, was a speakeasy that, according to legend, did not admit Jews. The future head of CBS, William Paley, who was barred because of his faith, vowed revenge. According to the story that circulated among CBS employees, Paley got revenge when he bought the building in which the speakeasy had been located years earlier and razed it. In its spot he built Paley Park, named after his mother. Some years later, Paley bought land next to his favorite club, '21,' to be used for the Museum of Television and Radio, one of his pet projects.

To make their speakeasy stand out among all these competitors, Jack and Charlie spared no expense in creating the kind of place in which their wealthy customers would feel at home. The upstairs dining rooms featured velvet banquettes, white table linens, and

crystal chandeliers. Downstairs, the bar (to this day, with no bar stools) was done in the style of an English men's club, with dark wood paneling, and in the rear was a small room with eight tables. The menu and prices that were to make '21' famous were put in place and were done with the purpose of keeping out cheapskates and rowdies. '21' was the only speakeasy on 52nd that didn't offer music, either. Conversation was the background to the dining experience here.

In order to assure that they'd never be raided again, Jack and Charlie hired architects and engineers to make their club virtually raid-proof. The iron grille on the front door, manned by doorman Jimmie Coslove, was the first line of defense. There was a vestibule inside fitted with four alarm buttons in case of a raid. If the alarm went off, the bartender would press a button that caused all the shelves holding liquor to collapse. The liquor would fall below into special chutes leading to the basement, where drains were fitted with rocks and sand so that not a drop of liquor would remain behind. All the cops would find in the basement would be broken glass. And you can't send a man to jail for broken glass.

Secret closets near the upstairs dining rooms held stashes of liquor. Hidden panels were activated by a switch in the metal coat rod, which, when touched by a metal hanger would cause panels to swing open and reveal a small room stocked with wine. In Summer 2004, during renovations to the third floor, a hidden vault was found, complete with uncashed checks and securities. The vault had been walled up for 40 years.

The biggest and most elaborate undertaking was construction of a door to a hidden room where '21' stored liquor and fine wines. After purchasing the house next door at #19, Jack and Charlie broke through the basement wall and had masons construct a false wall, on hinges, to create a hidden door leading to the basement of #19. The door, virtually undetectable, was built out of the same brick as the foundation, weighed over 4,000 pounds and was over a foot thick so that revenue agents wouldn't hear a hollow sound when tapping on the wall. The door opened only when a meat skewer was inserted into a tiny hole in the masonry, where the mechanism was buried. The hole was one of over a dozen drilled into the brickwork to fool anyone looking for a keyhole. Although there were many holes drilled, only one goes all the way to the lock deep inside. The door's mechanism was so well made that it has never failed and still works today.

One of the few patrons who knew about the hidden liquor warehouse in the cellar was Mayor Walker, who had his private booth built there. He entertained his girlfriend, the actress Betty Compton, in the booth, hidden from federal agents as well as his wife.

Once again the Mob tried to horn in on Jack and Charlie's operation. Soon after '21' opened, Legs Diamond announced he wanted "in." Once again, the Mob's dispatched thugs were dispatched by Jack and Charlie. Legs Diamond put a hit out on the two, but fortunately it was never carried out, as Diamond was bumped off himself over the weekend. This occurrence was a lucky break, not only for Jack and Charlie, but also for Ernest Hemingway. As H. Peter Kriendler wrote in his biography, *21: Every Day Was New Year's Eve*, Hemingway had had a tryst in '21' with Legs Diamond's girlfriend, and Diamond had also ordered a hit on the writer. So the course of New York City nightlife, as well as American literature, may have taken a very different turn if Diamond hadn't died that night.

Just before Prohibition ended, '21' was raided again. All the contraptions and precautions worked perfectly: the Feds spent over 12 hours poring over the place, poking and prodding, tapping on walls, and they found—nothing. Just fumes of alcohol and broken glass.

After Prohibition, the city's greatest and most elegant speakeasy made the happy transition into the city's greatest and most elegant eatery. In fact, as the War raged on, and the post-War boom hit midtown Manhattan, '21's' reputation as an expensive, exclusive eatery only grew. The club's reputation was helped by the star clientele and boosted by such exposure as Ed Sullivan's radio broadcasts from '21' during the War. When Humphrey Bogart has a regular table at your bar (Table 30), it's the kind of bar where a star can drink and eat and be undisturbed because he's just one of the crowd of celebrities. For who was Bogie compared to Eisenhower, Churchill, or Howard Hughes?

In fact, '21' has served as the New York White House, having accommodated Presidents Truman, Eisenhower, Kennedy, Nixon, Ford, Carter, Reagan, Bush, and Clinton. Restaurant manager Bruce Snyder has the tie clip and cuff links from Presidents Reagan and George H. W. Bush to prove it, too.

The years brought great profits and the need to expand. The walls were pushed through to #19 and #17 on either side. A sauna and gym were added on the third floor, and the men's club atmosphere was enhanced with services such as obtaining tickets for the theater or opera, providing a masseuse on call, and arranging for dry cleaning. As Pete Kriendler recalled, a customer "summed up the '21' experience: 'Everyone who comes in through the door is treated like a person who has not yet had his morning coffee.'" Not a bad way to run a saloon.

The tables in the bar room were coveted by those who wanted to be seen and to see. Where the maitre d' sat you had a lot to do with your importance, and being seated in "Siberia," the farther reaches of the downstairs dining room, was anathema to any star. Banishment was a barometer of your success. You sat in Siberia on the way up or on the way down in your career, but never at the height of your success. For the non-famous, it was all good, for every night guaranteed star sightings. One evening in the late 1930s, for example, '21' played host to Joan Bennett, Cary Grant, Katharine Hepburn, Tallulah Bankhead, Edward G. Robinson, Norma Shearer, Clark Gable, Charles Laughton, Leslie Howard, Joan Crawford, Myrna Loy, and Irene Dunne. And that was just the movie stars. It doesn't count the merely rich.

> *The tables in the bar room were coveted by those who wanted to be seen and to see. Where the maitre d' sat you had a lot to do with your importance...*

With the rich and famous came a menu to match. In addition to traditional cuisine, there were unusual dishes to tempt the captain of industry or visiting prince: caviar, pheasant, grouse, bear, partridge, wild boar, and terrapin. Game was often shot by celebrity hunters such as Robert Ruark or Frank Buck. The finest vintages, the oldest cognacs, the best Cubans. Wine was bought by patrons and stored in the '21' cellar, and the private stocks covered Presidents, stars, writers, and sports celebrities. Today, a tour of the wine room's private stock shows bottles belonging to Jimmy Stewart (who bequeathed them to friends to drink when at '21'), Richard Nixon (the bottles were a gift of Frank Sinatra), Elizabeth

JONES DAY
No Smoking
FULL of GOOD FELLOWSHIP at the PUNCHEON GROTTO 21 W 52
JACK THE BARON OF "21"
"21"

Taylor, and Ivan Boesky, as well as a bottle left by Chelsea Clinton's parents for her 21st birthday.

The customers loved their club and added what decor they could, bringing back souvenirs from world travels or big game hunts. John Hay "Jock" Whitney and Alfred Vanderbilt provided the first of several jockey figures, which became the symbol of '21.' Airline moguls, including Howard Hughes, donated scale models of airplanes, still hanging from the ceiling, as are many other items: race cars, boats, an elephant's tusk, Jackie Gleason's pool stick from "The Hustler," and a souvenir bullet from Teddy Roosevelt's Rough Riders.

By now, '21' has passed into legend. It has become one of the most famous bars in the world, and its kitchen is as praised as its barroom. The Kriendler brothers, all except Pete, had died by 1974. Pete finally sold '21' in the 1980s to Marshall Cogan, who sold it to the current owners, who operate Orient-Express Hotels, Trains & Cruises.

Bruce Snyder, the first nonfamily person hired for management, has been at '21' for 37 years. Talking about the average customer, he smiles, realizing as he names them that they are well above average. To him the pleasure comes from watching the celebrities mix with regular people. A famous Wall Street broker sitting next to a woman from New Jersey who is out for her anniversary, a descendent of President Polk brushing past Michelle Pfeiffer, no matter who comes through the iron gate, they are all treated with the respect and service that is '21's' hallmark. Simply put, the customer is number one at '21.' "It's a prejudiced comment, but we probably get the best clientele in the world, " says Snyder. With the Republican Convention in town in 2004, a party at '21' included former President and First Lady, George H.W. Bush and Barbara Bush, Vice President Dick Cheney and Lynne Cheney, and Donald Rumsfeld. Secret Service outside numbered over 200, and inside over 50. As '21' Public Relations Manager Diana Biederman says, every day is exciting at '21' because "you're seeing history pass through your doors."

# Bemelmans Bar

Carlyle Hotel
35 East 76th Street

*Ducking into Bemelmans Bar in the Carlyle Hotel, you get the feeling you've been there before. It must be the murals by Ludwig Bemelmans, creator of the Madeline series of children's books and one-time resident of The Carlyle.*

But there's more to it than the artwork. Bemelmans Bar has a cozy and glowy atmosphere, like a tea room out of an old novel. The Carlyle is that kind of hotel, and Bemelmans is that kind of room. The soft seats, the warm lighting, the butler-like service that you get only in an Old World-style hotel. If only life were this perfect all the time.

This jewel of a room is one of New York's treasures and a good example of what the Upper East Side is all about: the thick-carpet quiet and simple elegance that feels comfortable, not formal. That's just the sense the original owner was going for. Moses Ginsberg (whose daughter Diana named the hotel after essayist Thomas Carlyle) built the hotel as a residential hotel. With architecture by Sylvan Biren and interior design by Dorothy Draper, the hotel was a great example of Art Deco at its most restrained. Ginsberg owned The Carlyle until the 1940s, when millionaire Robert Dowling bought it. At that time it was run more like a private club, with social references necessary to stay or live there. Such measures kept the guest list on the heavyweight side. A prominent Democrat, Dowling entertained President Truman and other political notables. Longtime Bartender Tommy Rowles remembers when Truman stopped in and ordered an Old Grand-Dad on the rocks. Rowles, an avid beer drinker, commented that he could never drink something so strong as Old Grand-Dad. Whereupon Truman pointed to the gaggle of reporters waiting on the sidewalk and said, "If you had to walk 15 blocks with these guys following you, you'd drink this, too." But the president who loved The Carlyle the best was Kennedy. The Carlyle kept a duplex suite (and 55 cases of the president's private stock of wine in the cellar) for President Kennedy. The suite was kept empty just in case JFK

> *"If you had to walk 15 blocks with these guys following you, you'd drink this, too."*

decided to drop in. Bellman Michael O'Connell remembers saying goodbye to President Kennedy the last time Kennedy stayed at The Carlyle, just a week before his death.

Another famous resident was the author Ludwig Bemelmans. In exchange for room and board, Bemelmans painted murals in the Carlyle Bar, fanciful scenes of Central Park. For illustrations similar to the murals, Bemelmans earned the Caldecott Medal, awarded annually to the artist of the most distinguished illustration of children's books. Filled with peculiar charm, the murals feature the four seasons in Central Park, Madeline and her classmates, and a self-portrait of Bemelmans as a waiter, which was his occupation when he lived in Europe before he came to America. These works are the only public murals of Bemelmans that exist today.

In addition to its reputation as a bar, the Carlyle is famous for its music. The Café Carlyle, one of the city's most enduring and best loved cabaret rooms, is across the lobby from Bemelmans. New York legend Bobby Short was a staple there. Barbara Cook and Eartha Kitt also regularly perform there. At Bemelmans Bar, Barbara Carroll, a terrific jazz pianist, plays half the year, with Tony Bennett occasionally popping in to sing a song or two with Carroll. And when she's not playing, Peter Mintun is. Music has been in the Carlyle tradition since the day the hotel opened in 1930 and Richard Rodgers was the first tenant to live there. With the music and the date-friendly lighting, romantic success would seem guaranteed. The noise and bustle of Manhattan melt away, as you sink into the deep leather banquette and order your first drink.

With a cocktail menu designed by the legendary Dale DeGroff and the Carlyle's own Beverage Director Audrey Saunders, one drink might be the first of several. Like the dessert tray at a French restaurant, there are many artful temptations…the Jamaican Firefly, Whiskey Smash, or Champino. There are Slings, there are Mules, there are Sidecars, all these classic cocktails hearkening back to a day when a woman changed her drinks throughout the day just as she changed her handbag and shoes to suit the time and setting. According to Saunders, the drink menu was designed with the neighborhood and city as a backdrop. Says Saunders, "This is a quintessential New York watering hole; a real classic…" And Saunders knows her classics. She is herself a legendary mixologist, one who is devoted to creating cocktails with crystal-clear flavors and the purest of pedigrees, using vintage recipes and concocting her own potions. Her clientele appreciate her efforts. "They are still drinking Martinis, Manhattans, and Negronis as elegantly as they have been for the past 75 years," she comments. A nice picture, that.

*Like the dessert tray at a French restaurant, there are many artful temptations…the Jamaican Firefly, Whiskey Smash, or Champino.*

Just a few steps away from Central Park, Bemelmans Bar is a step into a slice of New York's tonier life on the Upper East Side. For those who imbibe too much, accommodations are part of the continuation of the perfect New York evening.

ONE WAY
ONE WAY
Bridge Café
Bridge Café
SINCE 1794

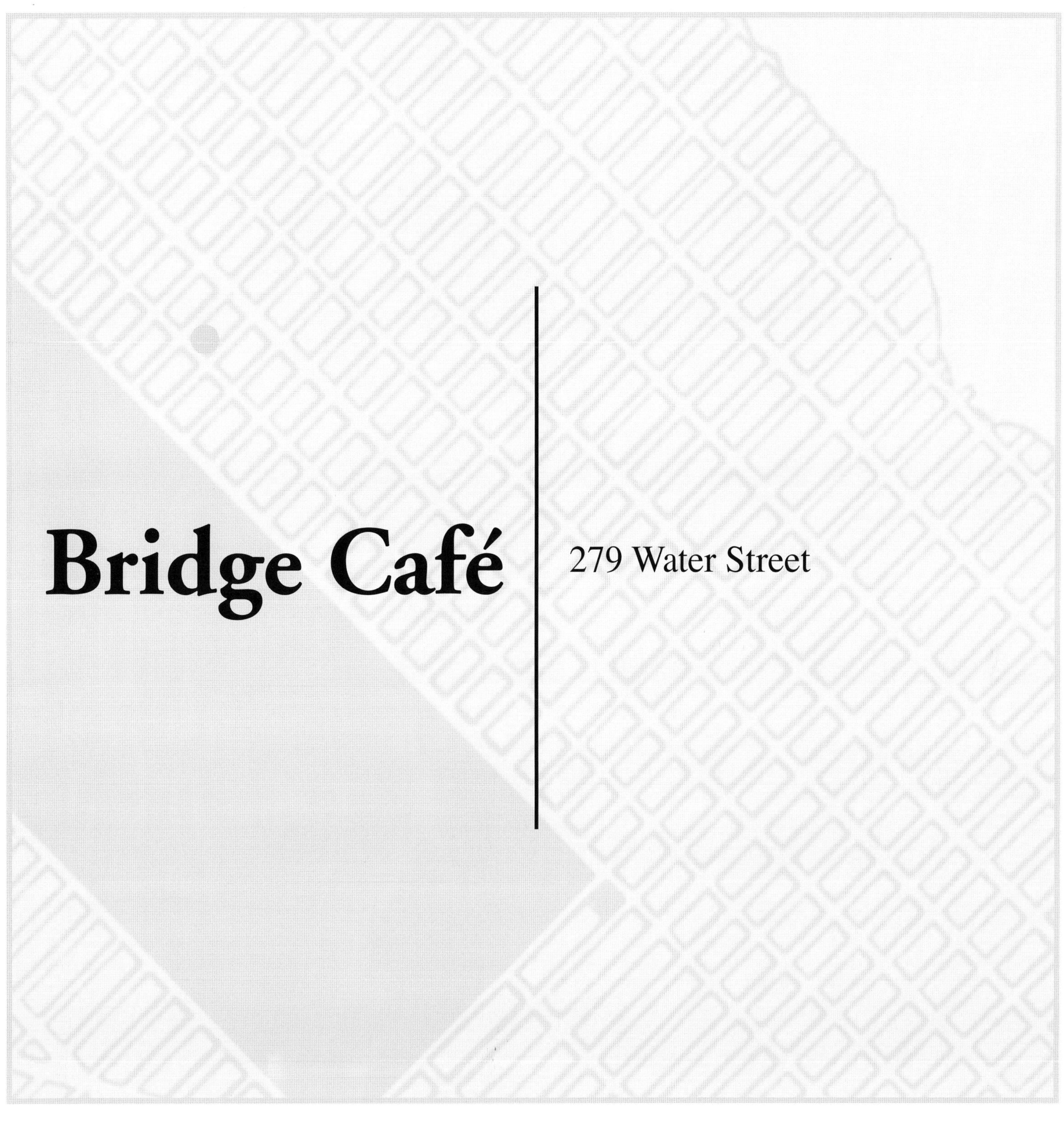

# Bridge Café

279 Water Street

WARNING
PORTO BARROS

*Wander along the South Street Seaport, where the Fulton Fish Market has been for over two hundred years, and you can see the vestiges of old New York.*

The New York of the fishermen, sailors, barrel makers, rope makers, and prostitutes who peopled what was once an active, noisy, smelly waterfront. A waterfront that was to become the busiest and richest in the world, one that would help create a city that also fit that description. A waterfront dotted with boarding houses, ale houses, and whore houses. And in the middle of it, New York's oldest continually-run business, Bridge Café.

In 1794, Newell Narme opened a "grocery and wine and porter bottler" in this building. From that day to this, liquor has been dispensed from this site, even illegally during Prohibition. There is a feud of sorts among bar aficionados in New York as to whether or not Bridge Café is indeed the oldest bar. Those who favor McSorley's feel that since that bar had a license to sell "near beer" during Prohibition, it was legally dispensing liquor during a period when Bridge Café was not. Therefore, The Bridge can't claim to have been continually selling liquor since 1794. However, most people don't seem to take Prohibition any more seriously now than they did when it was a law, so they don't really count those years as being dry ones. And so, by most accounts, Bridge Café is the oldest bar in New York.

Like many waterfront bars, Bridge Café has a notorious history. Reading through the lists of former owners and tenants, the difference between boarding house and bawdy house begins to blur. Various indictments against landlords for operating a disorderly house, (a nineteenth century euphemism for bordello), as well as a listing from the 1855 census showing the prostitutes in residence at 279 Water Street, make the point neatly. Sailors were shanghaied from bars like this, or robbed and rolled into the East River. History books recount some of the colorful figures from this neighborhood, among them a Dutchwoman who lived across the street. She kept company with sailors home on shore leave, the "deep water sailors" whose leave was longer than the common fisherman's. Her friends, in turn, left her various souvenirs, among them exotic animals such as a parrot and a monkey.

The bar went through many hands, and during the mid-nineteenth century was called the Empire House. The business was bought in 1859 by Thomas Norton, who ran it until 1881. Reform lawyer Frank Moss wrote, in 1897, that Norton's place was "filled with river pirates and Water Street hags." The poor lived so cramped along the docks that tuberculosis was rampant here, and the streets along Water and Dover were called "The Lung Blocks" in the nineteenth Century. During the construction of the Brooklyn Bridge, which was completed in 1883, some of the old tenements were torn down, to the relief of reformers like Moss. But Bridge Café remained in business, serving and housing the masons and ironworkers who built the bridge.

*Reform lawyer Frank Moss wrote, in 1897, that Norton's place was "filled with river pirates and Water Street hags."*

Through the turn of the twentieth century, the place had several owners, including a prominent city alderman, Jeremiah Cronin. By 1922, the saloon was sold to the McCormack family, and it was called McCormack's until the current owners bought it in 1979. By the early twentieth century, the upstairs rooms were no longer used as a brothel, and had been converted to a rooming house.

Former upstairs resident Nick Padula remembers his childhood over McCormack's, where his dad was cook from 1959 to 1967. There was no hot water and no tub in the apartment on the third

O'Reilleys $7.25
PINOT GRIS '04 Oregon
Clos La Chance $8.50
SAUVIGNON BLANC '03
Lambert Bridge $9.00
Chardonnay 03,CA
WARNING
PORTO

floor, so Nick and his three siblings bathed in their neighbor Mamie's apartment on the second floor. "Every night, we kids would come down to the bar in our...pajamas, and the old sailors would be in here. There wasn't anyone drinking in here that was under 50," Padula smiles, adding, "They were great to us, though. They let us play pool with them, and cards." He and his sisters and brother played along these streets and in the warehouses located in the pilings of the Brooklyn Bridge. There was wheat stored there, and peanuts, and tires, remembers Padula. "The Brookhattan Tire Company...," he says, "We used to sneak in there all the time and play." Brooklyn Bridge designer John Roebling had included these warehouses in the support structure of the bridge with the idea that the Fulton Fish Market would eventually be moved there. Some businesses did use the space as storage, but the idea never took off, and by the 1970s the rooms were abandoned.

Padula remembers a tough neighborhood, in the midst of the infamous Fish Market, long under investigation for its links to organized crime. "My dad owed the loansharks, and every Friday they'd come to the corner outside the bar at three, on the dot. I can still see them in their fedoras, with the brims pulled down over their faces. He'd meet them and pay them, every week. The mob guys, they'd come each week to the neighborhood, too, for their protection money. Everybody paid them, and if they didn't...." He pauses. "Once, I saw a guy who owed protection money get a fishhook right through his hand, as a warning...Another time,

I was looking out my bedroom window and saw a guy get shot in the head, right across the street. His eye was hanging out on the sidewalk." Padula points to a spot ten feet from the crime scene. "And right there, stood two cops, with their backs turned the whole time." He shrugs. "Things are different now that John [Gotti] is gone." Less corrupt, certainly. Less colorful, too. Some of that local color seeped into *The French Connection*, for it was at McCormack's that the real Popeye Doyle drank, and where he insisted the bar scenes be filmed.

Owner Adam Weprin's father bought McCormack's in 1979—by accident. The family had long been in real estate, but had never owned a bar. A misplaced ad in the *New York Times* caught his dad's eye. He bought it on what Weprin affectionately calls, "a bizarre whim, sheer insanity." The family has owned it ever since. They renamed it and spruced it up a bit—the interior was last renovated in 1886. (The bar itself dates from 1905 and is more Mission-style than Victorian.)

In 1979, when they were digging out part of the cellar to put in a walk-in refrigerator, a wall was demolished. One of the waitresses put on chef's whites and told Weprins's father, "I'm going excavating." He laughed at her until she sifted from the whitewash and rubble some artifacts—a leather button, a silver shoe buckle, a musket ball, lead shot, some clay fragments, and the remains of a house pipe. Weprin explains, "The house pipe was kept behind the bar. Someone who wanted to smoke would ask the barkeep for the house pipe and they'd give it to him. The pipestem was marked off where each smoker should break it off when he was done, so there was a clean mouthpiece for the next smoker." The house pipe found in the basement of Bridge Café has three marks left on its stem. The draw hole is very small, leading Weprin to wonder if opium was smoked in it. While these finds have historic interest, they were not the first objects uncovered. Weprin says that the workmen who broke through the wall must have found (and intended to keep) some things of value, for they told him, "We found something, but we can't tell you what it is."

Amazingly, there has never been a fire here, although there have been floods. Most noteworthy was the Nor'easter of December 1992. While Bridge Café was spared, Weprin remembers all the fish from the Fulton Fish Market were lost that day. "Hundreds and hundreds of fish were floating in the street. I passed a car and the water came halfway up the door. I heard this 'bump-bump' sound and saw a huge striped bass floating in the water next to the car, hitting its door. Just then, I see this guy from Chinatown with a shopping cart, and he comes up and looks around, sees nobody, puts the fish in his basket and takes off with it," he laughs. "I guess he served it at his restaurant that night. At least it didn't go to waste."

*Hundreds and hundreds of fish were floating in the street. I passed a car and the water came halfway up the door.*

The Bridge Café that Weprin runs is a romantic, quiet spot down under the Brooklyn Bridge. The menu is simple and elegant, and the kitchen has a good reputation. There are occasional mysterious footsteps on the ceiling, suggesting ghosts. But overall, it's a much quieter place than it was a hundred or two hundred years ago. It's a place that is comfortable with its history. It is neither burdened, nor overly excited by it. Rather, it seems to stand comfortably next to it, as it does to the bridge for which it was named. Not in the shadow of history, but with a nice view of it.

# Bull and Bear Steakhouse & Bar

540 Lexington Avenue
at 49th Street
Inside the Waldorf-Astoria Hotel

*The Bull and Bear is the place where businessmen traditionally got their basic four: martinis, cigars, beef, and stock market news.*

Some things have changed, most notably the addition of businesswomen, the banning of cigars, and the replacement of the old ticker tape machine in the bar with an electronic variety. Still, the martinis are arguably the best in Manhattan, and the steaks are legendary. The Bull and Bear was the first restaurant on the Eastern Seaboard to serve the Prime grade of Certified Angus Beef®. (Not just the first in New York City, but on the whole Eastern Seaboard!) They had it before any supermarket or butcher's shop did. This dedication to beef that is truly inspiring enables the Bull and Bear to hold its own in a city that prides itself on having the best of everything. Its location in the Waldorf-Astoria Hotel ensures a level of service that competing steakhouses have to contend with, and even if they can compete as far as service, they can't match this bar's history. Who else has played host to every star and statesman since the turn of both the twentieth and twenty-first Centuries? It's the Waldorf-Astoria. Hard to match, hard to beat.

This isn't the first bar at the Waldorf. There was a bar in its initial location, currently the site of the Empire State Building. When the Waldorf opened in its current location in 1931, it was at that time the largest hotel in the world. Today it remains if not the largest, certainly one of the most famous. Taking up a block of prime real estate between Park and Lexington Avenues, it is an Art Deco masterpiece.

The Men's Bar—dark, paneled, and for men only—functioned as a club for executives as well as stockbrokers. It was for them that the bronze statues of the bull and the bear, which held court on the bar for years, had such meaning. In 1960, amid fanfare, the current bar opened. Renamed the Bull and Bear, the most significant thing about it was neither the Bull nor the Bear, but the women–allowed to drink here for the first time. Actress Jessica Tandy cut the ribbon on opening day, and her colleague, Hermione Gingold, crossed the threshold first and was the first woman served here.

(Women were allowed only after three p.m. at that time, and with an escort.) Today, escort-free female powerbrokers and ladies who lunch enjoy the service and ambience–still decidedly masculine and clubby. In fact, before smoking was banned in New York City, the maitre d'hotel would ask female patrons upon seating them if "Madame would like a cigar after dinner?", an exercise in equality, if not futility.

*Today, escort-free female powerbrokers and ladies who lunch enjoy the service and ambience–still decidedly masculine and clubby.*

The bar itself is mahogany, a nod to the original bar at the old Waldorf, which was a massive mahogany and rosewood affair. That bar was taken apart and small pieces of it given away as souvenirs when Prohibition forced the closing of the Men's Bar. At the Bull and Bear, the pentagonal bar is in the center of the room, a configuration hearkening back to Victorian times. Two bartenders usually work both sides, and many of the staff, like Oscar Estrada, a 35-year veteran, have been here for decades. He looks after his customers, just as his former colleague, the legendary Oscar Tschirky ("Oscar of the Waldorf"), did. The modern-day Oscar receives Christmas cards from regulars who are out of town, and is so trusted by patrons that it's not uncommon for people to send mail to regulars "care of Oscar." Who are his favorites of all the celebrities who have starred at functions here or stayed at the hotel? He can't begin to name them all. Frankly, the regulars (some who have been patrons here for more than thirty years) are just as important to him. "To me, everybody's important, everybody's famous," says Estrada. This kind of service and this classic setting is probably what prompted the *New York Times* to name the Bull and Bear as one of the world's three greatest classic bars.

# Cedar Tavern

82 University Place

CEDAR
CEDAR

*Not many bars have college courses named after them — but* **this is** *the Cedar Tavern.*

Now, "legend" is a word that gets tossed about all too frequently, but the fact that New York University has a course titled "Cedar Tavern and After: 1950s Art in New York," justifies its use in this case. The Cedar is, simply, a legend.

It's fitting that the opening shot in *Requiem for a Heavyweight* was a slow pan of the now 140-year-old bar, when it was in the Susquehanna Hotel. The bar is gorgeous, with the back bar heavily carved and inlaid with mirrors and stained glass. Thankfully it was saved from the wrecking ball by owner Joe Diliberto's dad and uncle (founders Sam Diliberto and his brother in law, John Bodnar).

If you're like most visitors, you'll go to the Cedar because of who went there before you. Ask Joe. He'll smile and reel off a list that sounds like roll call at the New York School. And in fact, it is.

Joe Diliberto has been here since he was a kid and started out helping his father and his uncle behind the bar. Not serving drinks, of course, but cleaning. "I used to clean the top of the back bar. The bartenders would toss their small change up there; they didn't want it. So my dad would lift me up and I'd dust up there, and I got to keep what I found," Joe remembers. This is perhaps the special hidden charm of the Cedar. It was, and is, a family-owned business and a neighborhood bar. Sam, a butcher, and John, a window washer, saved up their own small change and bought the place in 1955 from Smokey Joe Provenzano, (who, despite the exotic nickname, was not in the Mafia). "It's a painter's bar," the elder

*Sam, a butcher, and John, a window washer, saved up their own small change and bought the place in 1955 from Smokey Joe Provenzano…*

Diliberto told his son. Joe thought he meant house painters. In fact, he meant artists, as in some of the greatest painters the century produced. Willem de Kooning, Franz Kline, Mark Rothko, Robert Motherwell, and Red Grooms were all regulars at the Cedar, through its various incarnations from its original name (Cedar Street Tavern) to a couple of moves, lastly from 8th Street to University Place. And then there was Jackson Pollock, who loved the Cedar, and held court there nightly (though his lover, Ruth Kligman, called the place "that crummy bar.")

Cheap beer (25 cents, which even beatniks could afford) and friendly owners and staff made it the artist's hangout, sort of an Our Gang clubhouse, only with poetry readings and lots and lots of liquor—the better to write or read poetry with. Allen Ginsberg, Gregory Corso, Jack Kerouac, LeRoi Jones, Frank O'Hara, and even Bob Dylan got inspiration in liquid form here. Red Grooms immortalized the scene in his Cedar Bar series, and writer Dawn Powell used the Cedar as a basis for the cafe in her novel *The Golden Spur*, which Gore Vidal called "the New York novel." They all came there, all those who figured in the Beat Generation: the legendary painters, writers, and musicians, as well as the local Village characters you've never heard of unless you lived in the Village at that time. The legends. The heavyweights.

> *Allen Ginsberg, Gregory Corso, Jack Kerouac, LeRoi Jones, Frank O'Hara, and even Bob Dylan got inspiration in liquid form here.*

Tom Wolfe, in *The Painted Word*, called the Cedar the scene of the "cénacle des cénacles." Roughly translated, it means the inner circle of inner circles. But the word "cénacle" comes from the Old French and originally meant the upper room where the Last Supper took place. One can imagine Pollock, the quintessential temperamental artist, preferring this meaning to the contemporary one.

Famous artists and writers aside, the Cedar is just a good neighborhood bar. All kinds of people have always felt comfortable here. That feeling has to do with the location, in the heart of a student and artist colony, and with the way the place is run. As John Bodnar once told his nephew, "We're in the business of good will." And so, yes, famous painters did hang out here. But so did ordinary folks from the neighborhood; this was their place, too. That guy over there, who stopped in for coffee—he's been coming here forty years. Uncle John was right. The secret to being popular and sticking around is respect. Good will. Joe and his manager of 23 years, Richard Schimenti, protect the famous customers from curious onlookers. But they extend the same kind of courtesy to the locals, too. And given the locale, the locals are an unusual bunch.

Like the time during the Blackout of '79, when Joe put candles all over to light the place, and one of his regulars, who was a little unsteady on his feet at the time, caught fire while relieving himself in the restroom. Fortunately just the lights, and not the water, were out, and they got to him in time. In fact, they haven't lost a customer yet at the Cedar. And given the propensity for artists and writers to get a bit unsteady on their feet, we're all grateful to them for that.

BRASS CANNON

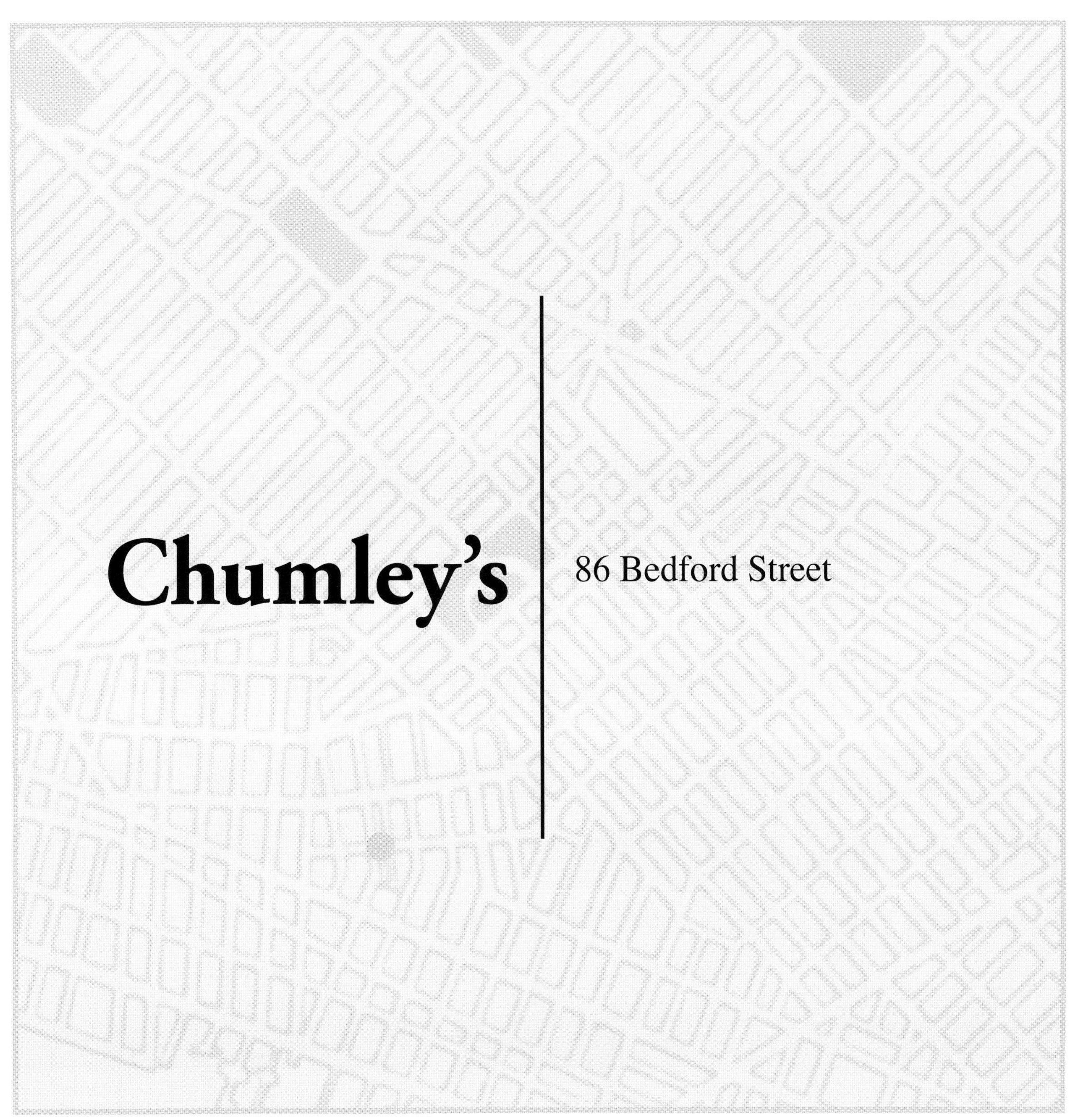

# Chumley's

86 Bedford Street

86

*Just getting into Chumley's is an adventure. The last surviving genuine speakeasy in New York, Chumley's has no sign out front, and to make matters more confusing, there are two doors marked 86 Bedford Street, so one may (as often happens) go traipsing up the wrong steps by mistake.*

But you won't mind; nobody seems to, not even the folks who live at the other 86 Bedford Street. They're used to the confusion, after all, confusion is part of the fun, and part of the reason Chumley's is still here today. Confusion helped the original tenants stay one step ahead of the law.

Blessed with two entrances, one at 86 Bedford, the other on Pamela Court, a hidden courtyard off Barrow Street, Chumley's was known as "the place on Bedford," back in a time when speakeasy addresses were closely guarded secrets, traded with the kind of care that should have been used for the Stock Market. The place was founded by Leland "Lee" Chumley, a character whose character has been the subject of some speculation over the years. A soldier of fortune and a "Wobblie" (a member of the IWW, a Socialist labor union), Chumley had been manager of the Black Knight, a speakeasy over on MacDougal Street. In 1926, he bought the property on Bedford and published a newsletter and held IWW meetings upstairs, eventually taking over the blacksmith's shop downstairs to run as his own speakeasy. The building had been in continuous use as a blacksmith's since 1820, and the double archway is still visible in Chumley's, as well as the forge (although it was redone into a fireplace when Lee bought it). Some people say that he ran a bordello or gambling parlor upstairs, and there are some bits of evidence to support that, such as the dumbwaiter that goes to the second floor, big enough to fit two people, or the remnants of an electric buzzer system. Whatever went on upstairs is a mystery, but the operations downstairs are legendary.

"The place on Bedford" was a popular speakeasy and Lee Chumley was a popular man in the West Village throughout Prohibition. The place was packed nightly and was a favorite with writers. After the wedding reception for Zelda and Scott Fitzgerald, the party moved on to Chumley's where, sometime in the early morning, Zelda and Scott were rumored to have consummated their marriage at table 7, that booth by the fireplace.

Chumley's was also the birthplace of the term "86." Anyone who's worked in a restaurant knows that this expression means an item is no longer available or a patron is no longer desired. When the cops would very kindly call ahead before a raid, they'd tell the bartender to "86" his customers, meaning they should scram out the 86 Bedford door, while the police would come to the Pamela Court entrance. Just in case, there were two other secret exits, one in the kitchen and one behind the bar, both still hidden in the tile work. The dumbwaiter and two trap doors leading to the cellar were also pressed into use during raids.

And so Chumley's merrily floated along during Prohibition, until it ended in 1933. Lee was third in line to get his liquor license the day it ended.

Life was good to Lee Chumley. He had the perfect bachelor's existence: a great bar, tons of friends, and an apartment in the Village. Plenty of cash and lots of pretty girls to spend it on. But life was short for Lee, and in 1935 he died suddenly of a heart attack. And then the story gets *really* interesting.

*But life was short for Lee, and in 1935 he died suddenly of a heart attack. And then the story gets* **really** *interesting.*

Henrietta Chumley had been married to Lee for years and kept their home out in Brooklyn. She knew that her husband had a business in town, but she was a little sketchy on what exactly that business was until she inherited it. Meanwhile, Chumley's employees, customers, friends, and "associates" had no idea he'd been married. One of the bartenders, Lee's right hand man, figured he'd get the place when Lee died. He was surprised, along with half of the neighborhood's female

population, the day plump, short, 42-year-old Henrietta Chumley showed up. She'd never worked in a bar before, let alone run one. Nobody thought she'd last a year. Turns out she lasted longer than any of the owners, before or since. She ran the bar from 1935 until her death in 1960. Every night she'd sit at her favorite table (Scott and Zelda's favorite, too), playing solitaire and drinking Manhattans 'til she passed out, the party continuing around her. Come closing time, the waiters would carry her upstairs to her apartment and pour her into bed. One morning, they went to take her up, but then they realized she had already "ascended." Henrietta had spent most of the evening dead in her seat.

Don't be fooled, though, by the idea that Henrietta was inattentive to her business. (She kept a close eye on the place—for most of the night, anyway). And she seemed to have had an innate ability to play to people's vanity. She had the tiny staircase installed at the Bedford door so women could make "an entrance" when they came in. And her best move of all was starting the tradition of displaying the dust jackets of all the books published by writers who drank at Chumley's. And there were plenty: Hemingway, O'Neill, Fitzgerald, Miller, Mailer, Steinbeck, Dos Passos, de Beauvoir (who wrote of Chumley's, "It has that rare thing in America: an atmosphere!"), Styron, Cheever, Talese, Nin, Kerouac, Corso, Ginsberg, Dreiser, Cummings, Faulkner, and Salinger.

In fact, the plaque over the fireplace subtly states the significance of the establishment among writers, commemorating the day in 2000 that Friends of Libraries USA designated Chumley's a Literary Landmark.

Regardless of its landmark status, Chumley's is a favorite fixture in the Village for tourists and locals. It has a private club feel without the snobbery of a private club. It enjoys the loyalty of its regulars, who include firefighters from Engine Company 24, Ladder Company 5, a firehouse that lost 11 men on 9/11. Memorials have been held here, with firefighters coming from as far away as Oklahoma and Toronto, their graffiti on the chimney and the scarred tables.

Chumley's has the character of a place of long history, with the secret entrance and nooks and crannies. There are also the great beers and ales, all brewed locally. Watching people enter after their search for the door or  seeing the bartenders change the kegs is especially entertaining. Changing a keg requires opening a trap door in the floor and lowering the keg on a pulley to the cellar. Manager of 10 years, Gina Ruiz, stands guard to make sure nobody falls through. The fireplace occasionally spits out flaming cinders that are extinguished by the bartenders using seltzer siphon bottles. Watching over this quirky scene is Chef Suyu, who's been with Chumley's for 40 years and whose portrait hangs in the dining room. In the midst of the confusion, though, there is a mission. Or, as Steve Shlopak, owner for the past 18 years, remarks, "We think of ourselves as stewards—husbanding this place for the time being. We plan to be here for quite a while, but we know Chumley's itself will go on far longer."

CORNER
BISTRO
CORNER BISTRO

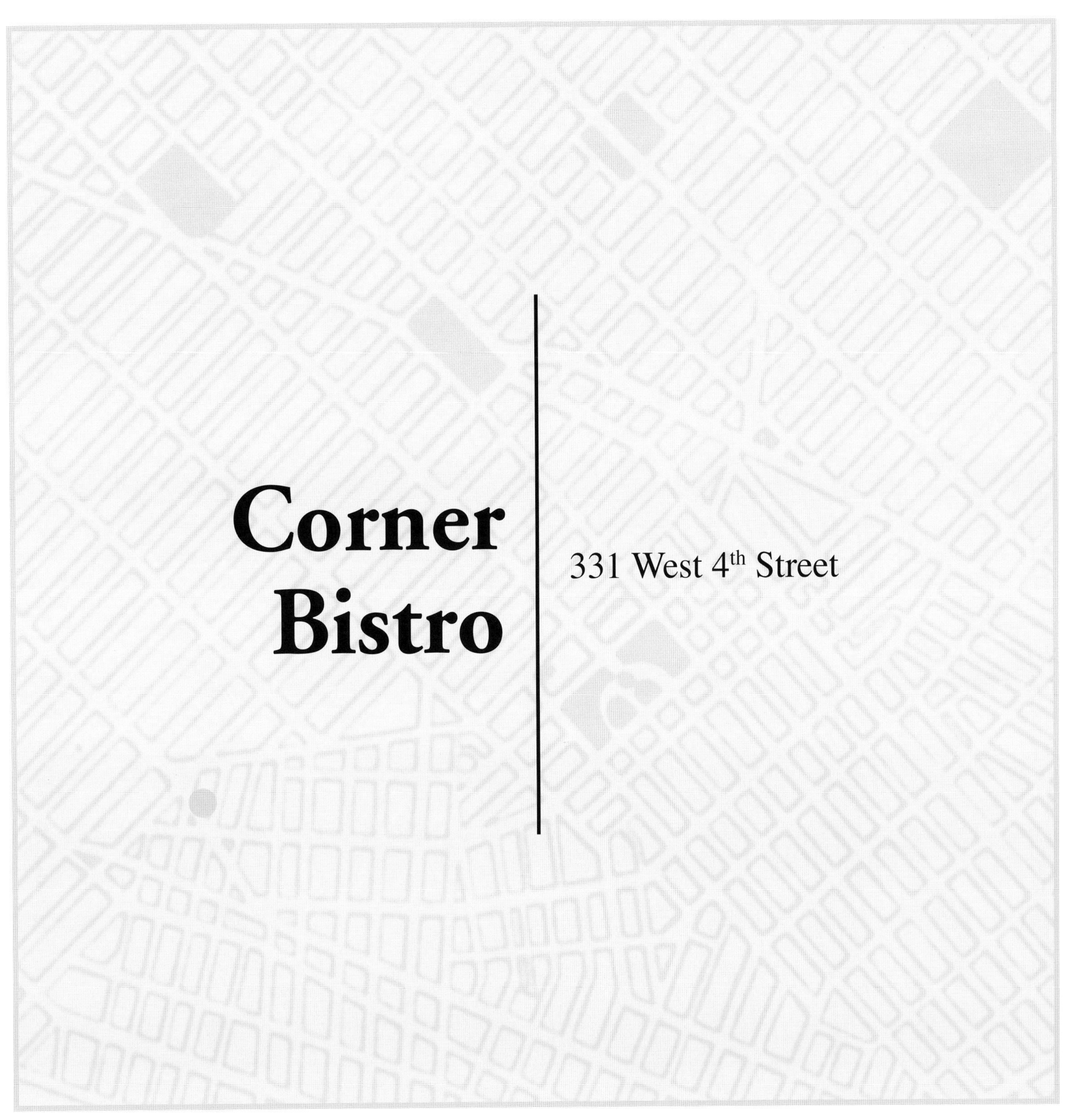

# Corner Bistro

331 West 4$^{th}$ Street

*When you talk about a place like Corner Bistro, you're talking about a corner of New York City history.*

The building has been here since 1827, back when only structures on corners were permitted by fire code to use clapboard and timber. Take a walk around to the back alley, and you can still see the original wooden wall.

If these beer and history soaked timbers could talk, their story would start back in the day when the West Village was a pretty rough neighborhood. Just off the docks, it was a place where longshoremen and merchant seamen lived and work, drank and fought. These were the days of "rushing the growler," when kids would be sent down to the corner to fetch pop's beer with a tin pail. This pail the barman would fill, the rim rubbed with butter or grease to keep the head from foaming too much. In these times, the Corner Bistro would be packed on a Sunday after church, with baby carriages lined up all along the outside.

Around the turn of the twentieth century, Rupert's Brewery came and put in the bar, complete with top-of-the-line ice boxes and electric lights. Nicked and worn, the bar still stands today. Its inner workings, however, have been updated.

Then came Prohibition, when a well-known Village family, the O'Briens, owned it, operating it as a butcher shop up front and a speakeasy in the back. (You can still see the cuts where they took the bar apart to allow them to bring it to the hidden saloon). This period was during the reign of bartender Barney McNicholls, who ran it illegally and then legally, from Prohibition through World War II. So tough he

*This period was during the reign of bartender Barney McNicholls, who ran it illegally and then legally, from Prohibition through World War II.*

was able to talk down a robbery at gun point, McNicholls was there the day old man O'Brien bet a patron that he could lift a full beer barrel (thirty-one gallons) onto the bar. Though in his 60s, O'Brien did it. Turned out to be the last bar bet he ever made though—he dropped dead of a heart attack afterwards.

*McNicholls was there the day old man O'Brien bet a patron that he could lift a full beer barrel onto the bar.*

McNicholls had each of his regulars paint a tin ceiling tile a different color and sign his name to it upon his return from World War II, turning the ceiling into a crazy patchwork of bright colors. Didn't matter, though, because only regulars drank there. The bar changed hands during the fifties, and became a gay bar called The Frisco. After a raid and subsequent closure under a morals charge, it looked as if a liquor license could not be used at this address ever again. A savvy businesswoman and writer, Tania de Gomez, who happened to be a friend of Nelson Rockefeller's, however, got around the paperwork and opened the Corner Bistro in 1961. Tania tried to run it as an authentic French bistro, but the idea never took. Yoko Ono tended bar here for a bit, but within a year Tania sold the bar, and by 1967, Bill O'Donnell took it over and has run it ever since. With his manager and bartender, Harold Wedick, they have seen a steady stream of Village people come and go–the famous, the infamous, and the anonymous. Gregory Corso made the Corner Bistro his hangout for years, James Baldwin did, too. It's been a favorite for anyone playing the Village Vanguard, including Art Blakey, Bobby Timmons, Zoot Sims, Miles Davis, and Charlie Mingus. Actors from HB Studio have practiced their lines and hoisted a few here, too, including Al Pacino, Robert De Niro, and Meryl Streep.

Long gone are the longshoreman, though their laughter still echoes through these narrow streets, presumably over the exorbitant real estate prices that the neighborhood commands. Today's patrons are locals, artists, writers, actors, and businesspeople, too. They share bar space with the likes of Sarah Jessica Parker and Matthew Broderick, F. Murray Abraham, and Liv Tyler. The beer still flows up from kegs in the cellar, the tables in the back room are covered with carved graffiti from generations of long nights, and the tiny grill fries up unapologetically meaty burgers that are rated among New York City's best.

ABC
WINTER RUG
SALE
75% off
ABC

# Dublin House

225 West 79$^{th}$ Street

DUBLIN
HOUSE
BAR
TAP ROOM
BAR
ORIENT
223 West 79th Street

*Irish bars once thickly populated the Upper West Side and spawned a generation of imitators. The Dublin House, though, is the real thing.*

This establishment is not a sawdust-and-suds Irish bar, or a soccer-flag-and-pint-waving place, either. It doesn't hit you over the head and yell "Erin Go Bragh!", but approaches you quietly and genially, and asks, "Would you like a pint, then?" There is a lilt to the voice and a friendly glint in the eye. It could be owner Chris Waters or his bartender of 11 years, Gerrard Daly. Go ahead, sit down, make yourself at home. Hospitality is the essence of a true Irish bar.

You don't have to be Irish to appreciate the Dublin House, but it helps. Spend time here and, if you're Irish, you may find yourself reminded of someone. Look around, at the bottles behind the bar and the porcelain figurines, without a speck of dust. The bar and the bathroom, old and worn, but scrubbed clean. (Dublin House is probably the cleanest bar in all Manhattan.) Suddenly you remember; ah yes, Uncle Kevin! (or whatever is the name of your Irish bachelor uncle)—this place sort of reminds you of him. A little courtly, a little threadbare, and very, very clean.

Locals and regulars have been here for years, as the neighborhood rode the roller coaster ride that characterized the Upper West Side. The bar was opened in 1933 by Waters's uncle John Carway when the Upper West Side was lined with residences and genteel hotels. Waters arrived from Ireland in 1947 and ended up tending bar here (a job that lasted for 42 years and included inheriting the place when his uncle died in 1978). In those days, Waters says, "A seven ounce glass of beer was 10 cents, a shot of rye whiskey was 35 cents." Scotch, always high-end, cost 60 cents a shot.

*Locals and regulars have been here for years, as the neighborhood rode the roller coaster ride that characterized the Upper West Side.*

During the fifties the neighborhood went to seed and the hotels became flophouses. Still, Waters had steady customers, the types usually down on their luck. Rather than run a tab, he'd front them a bit to tide them over till their checks came. "I broke even on that," he says. Most people were good to their word. One in particular, a regular, borrowed some money and then stopped coming in. Months went by, and Waters thought he'd never see his money again. He passed the guy in the park, Waters remembers, "And he says to me, 'I didn't forget you, Chris.'" Still, no money. Then months later came an envelope, from Detroit with the money paid in full, plus interest."

*Times got better at the end of the seventies, when real estate went crazy in New York.*

Times got better at the end of the seventies, when real estate went crazy in New York. The old apartments suddenly commanded huge rents, the hotels renovated or became co-ops. "In 1947, when I came here, those hotels would charge you $8.00 or $10.00 a week for a room, and they'd be glad to have you," Waters smiles. The prosperous eighties were the bar's best time, packed with college kids and yuppies. They were a new breed, not well steeped in bar culture. Daly laughs, "Every once in a while, someone would ask, 'When does the Irish dancing start?' They'd see the sign that says 'Tap Room,' and they'd think there was tap dancing here." Since the nineties, Dublin House has settled back into a more quiet profile. That's ok, you can have a decent conversation or read the paper. Because of this homey feel, Dublin House often turns up on "Best Bar" lists. The place was also awarded landmark status by the City of New York, for the building is a beautiful old late nineteenth century townhouse, and the sign outside, gorgeous with green and gold neon, is a work of art itself.

HOUSE
DUBLIN
BAR
TAP ROOM
BAR

GOD
BLESS
GARY

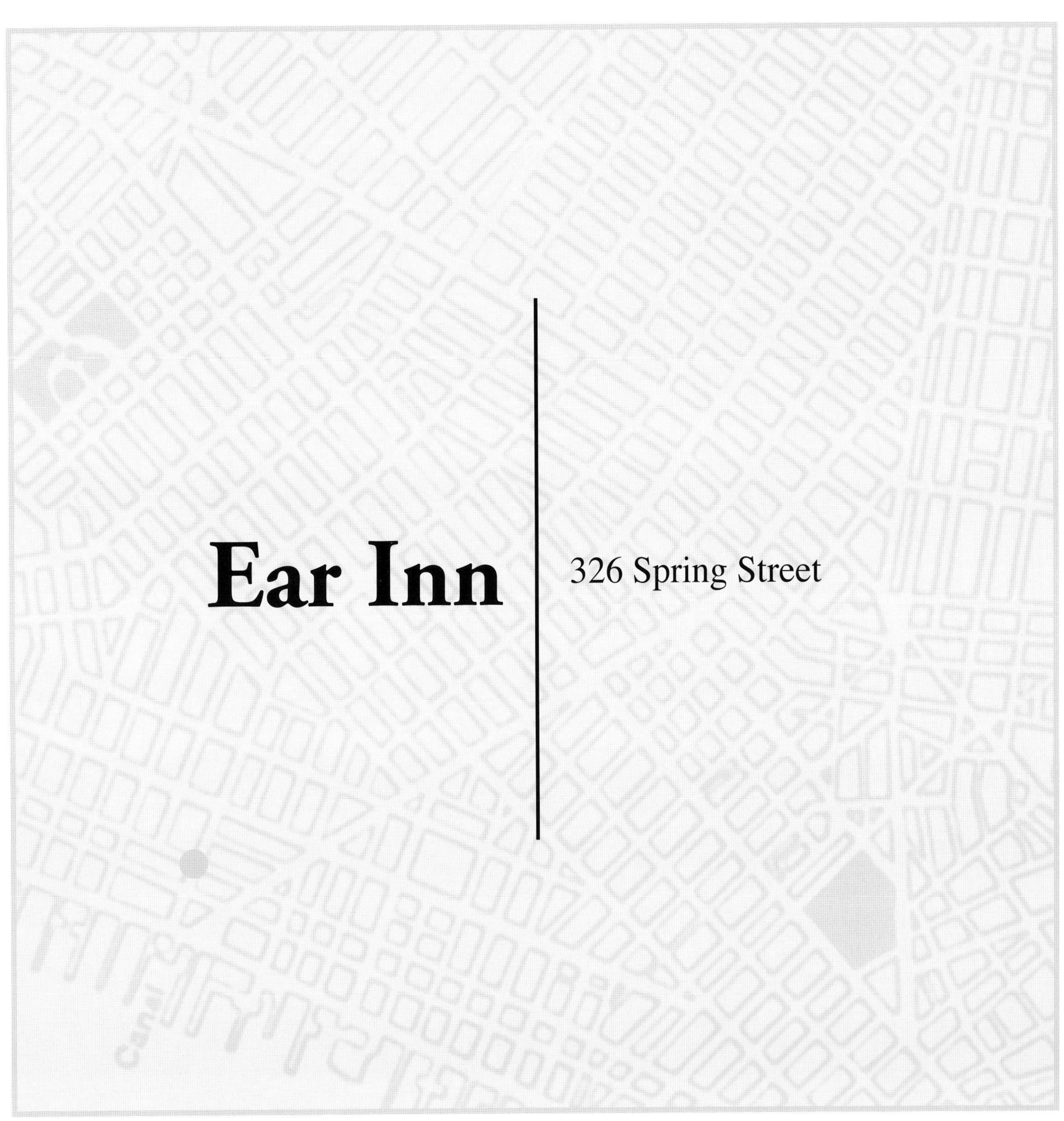

# Ear Inn

326 Spring Street

est 1817 A.D.
326
326
POST NO BILLS

*Dockside bars have a way of making you forget what coast you're on, even before you've had a drink.*

The atmosphere of the sea and sailing erase time and place in a way that's different from any other kind of bar, its history wrapping around you like the fog. The Ear Inn could be in San Francisco. But it is a true New York bar, full of true New York history. It has the pedigree to prove it, designated by the City's Landmark Commission and the National Register of Historic Places.

The Ear Inn is in a building known to historians as the James Brown House. One of the few remaining Federal-style houses in New York City, it was built in 1817 for James Brown, a free black and an aide to George Washington. (He may be pictured in Leutze's painting of *George Washington Crossing the Delaware.*) Brown, a successful tobacco trader, ran a tobacco shop downstairs and used the upper floors as living quarters. The house was right on the river then, though it is a block and a half from the water's edge today. Still, it's so close that the building's owner and local historian, Rip Hayman, told the *Downtown Express*, "We have to pump out the tide from the basement twice a day." The James Brown house is not far from where Washington's presidential mansion, the Richmond Hill Estate, once stood at the corner of Spring Street and Avenue of the Americas. (Richmond Hill was at other times home to John Adams and Aaron Burr.) At the time it was built, lower Greenwich Village was rural, Canal Street was a stream, and the area was covered in meadows and swamps.

*At the time it was built, lower Greenwich Village was rural, Canal Street was a stream, and the area was covered in meadows and swamps.*

After the War, and being close to the river, the area became increasingly commercial and was dependent on the seafaring trade.

Brown died, and according to Hayman, the building was first used as a bar around 1835. A sailor's bar, it was a place where no woman ventured unless she had business there (usually conducted upstairs). The building also served as a smuggler's den. Artifacts from this period unearthed during renovation include an old pistol found in the chimney—hidden in a hurry, no doubt. Today, the display of old whiskey jugs and bottles are a testament to centuries of fellowship and imbibing. During this time the bar was called The Green Door by its patrons (there was no sign), though it was owned by Thomas Cloke from 1888 to 1919 and officially called Cloke Bar and Grill. Its motto, "Known from Coast to Coast," persisted for more than a hundred years.

*Its motto, "Known From Coast to Coast," persisted for over a hundred years.*

Cloke sold the bar on the eve of Prohibition, though the law did little to restrict the activities going on there. After Prohibition, the neighborhood went through its ups and downs, floating like a buoy on the fortunes of the city and the waterfront. By the 1970s, it was almost deserted. The Washington Street Food Market, where ships from all over the world had unloaded spices and food for hundreds of years, moved to Jersey. The longshoremen and stevedores soon followed. The West Side Highway was being torn down and the World Trade Center was being built. The little old bar known as The Green Door stood battered and isolated in the wasteland. Then along came Rip Hayman, who rented the apartment upstairs while studying at Columbia University. In 1977 he bought the place with some friends. They published a music journal called *The Ear*, and they named the bar after that publication. They were able to simply paint over part of the B in the old neon sign, so that BAR said EAR. A neat trick that helped sidestep the quagmire of the City's Landmark Commission's regulations on signage, too.

Hayman and the Ear Inn have seen the stunning turnaround of the areas now known as SoHo and TriBeCa. The old dive beloved by sailors and longshoremen is now a favorite haunt of artists, poets, musicians, and yes, ghosts—especially one called Mickey. The bar is still divey, but that's the charm. It *is* a waterfront bar, after all. Not a fancy seafaring-themed bar, but a real dockside joint. Its memorabilia comes from ships, not shops. There are poetry readings and artists' openings, and people like David Byrne are interviewed for *Salon* here. The James Brown House has been lovingly preserved and protected by Hayman and friends, and the Ear Inn has flourished under the care of owners Sheridan and Walker and longtime bartenders George Peck (retired) and John Griffin. There's a terrific website about the house and the bar, as well as an excellent book about them by Alexander Coe. After all these years, the bar is still "known from coast to coast."

EAR
est 1817 A.D.

KID McCOY
JOE LOUIS
PAUL BERLENBACH

# Fanelli Cafe

94 Prince Street

FANELLI
CAFE
Bass
BEERS
ON DRAUGHT

*Located on a site where one person or another has been serving liquor since 1847 enables Fanelli Cafe to call itself the "second oldest continuous food and drink establishment" in New York City.*

Built at a time when Lower Manhattan was the center of the city and Fourteenth Street and above considered the countryside, Fanelli Cafe (known under various names until 1922) was part of a block of bordellos that operated along Mercer and Prince Streets. These bawdy houses, along with the ubiquitous gambling dens and saloons, catered to the city's political powerbrokers who worked down the street at City Hall. During the Civil War, Brooks Brothers, Tiffany, and Lord and Taylor, along with luxury hotels, moved onto lower Broadway, the Fifth Avenue of its day, bringing increased traffic to the area.

The business at 94 Prince Street thrived and expanded, and around this time the original wood structure was replaced by a brick building. The brothels had a neat system: ales dispensed downstairs, ails dispensed upstairs (at the brothel). Current Fanelli's owner Sasha Noe has several "artistic" photographs of the "girls upstairs" from this era. Taken in the bar downstairs, they testify to the days when the cafe was more like the Playboy Club than the family-friendly pub it is today.

In 1878, Nicholas Gerdes bought the grocery, as the business is sometimes referred to in census documents. (It was common in those days for groceries to sell alcoholic drinks.) His name is still etched in the glass transom over the door. Gerdes ran the place as a bar downstairs and leased the upstairs to various manufacturers, as well as the occasional lady of the evening. By this time the elegant shops and hotels were leaving the neighborhood, and warehouses and industries were moving in. These businesses built the decorous cast iron buildings that SoHo is known for, filling them with factories and workers. A hundred years later, the huge interior spaces behind these gorgeous facades would become magnets for artists seeking gallery and work space. But at the turn of the twentieth century, the neighborhood still had a long way to go until it became SoHo.

Gerdes owned the business until 1902, and then it changed hands twice before Michael Fanelli bought it in 1922. He ran the business for the next 60 years, and fortunately he never renovated the interior, keeping the Victorian decor as it was.

Fanelli Cafe stayed open throughout Prohibition, brewing bathtub gin and making wine in a hidden room behind the bar. (The room is still there, though inaccessible.) Of course, walk-ins and cops who weren't "friends of the establishment" were served nonalcoholic beverages only, but for regulars the soft drinks were decidedly hard. Located in the midst of a manufacturing district, Fanelli's did a brisk business, and it's pretty well known that the upstairs kept on its historic function as a bordello for some time. Michael Fanelli was a former boxer who promoted boxers and plastered the inside of the cafe with their photos. ("Promoted" is used loosely here to describe actual investments, as well as wagering on fights.) All in all, Fanelli's was a typical blue collar bar.

By the 1960s, manufacturing had left the neighborhood, and the lofts were abandoned. Artists began to rent out whole floors as living and work spaces. At first, Fanelli mistrusted the new crowd, but over time he began to like them, albeit begrudgingly. This artsy crowd appreciated the history of the neighborhood and the architecture and design of his cafe, reinforcing his sentimental feelings for the old place. When the time came to retire, his two sons were not interested in taking over, and Fanelli was stuck. Who would ensure that the building would stay standing and not be ripped down to make some fancy apartment building or store, now that the neighborhood, recently dubbed SoHo, was becoming so tony?

*Artists began to rent out whole floors as living and work spaces.*

The answer came in the person of Romanian immigrant Hans Noe. In 1982, Noe, who had lived in the neighborhood since 1947, offered to buy the business and building from Fanelli. After Noe guaranteed he would maintain architectural integrity, Fanelli agreed to sell.

Hans Noe's son, current owner Sasha Noe, grew up playing in the basement and helping out around the bar. It was a fun place to play and hang out. "There were these vaults underground in the basement," he says. His job one summer was to close them off. (The city had wanted to charge Noe a fee for using them, as they were located under the sidewalk.) Aside from complying with city regulations, Fanelli Cafe has barely changed since Noe bought it in 1982. Just as Michael Fanelli had done, both the Noes have kept the original fixtures and interior, which is no easy task, particularly when things break. It's hard to find repairmen who are also skilled with antiques, even in New York.

The years since Noe bought Fanelli Cafe have seen SoHo become SoHo. Today, even the artists can't afford to live here. They've essentially driven themselves out. (It's because of the galleries that rents skyrocketed and expensive stores moved in.) Fanelli's has stayed the same, although there are a fair amount of wealthy folks and celebs among the clientele. It's rare to hear a bar owner complaining about paparazzi, but this Sasha grew up here and misses the old days. "They [the paparazzi] hang outside and wait for someone to leave," sighs Noe. It's not easy being an authentic New York bar in the midst of this, but in a way, it's a return to the old days when lower Broadway was a glamorous shopping district. Only nowadays, the carriage trade drives Range Rovers, and the girls upstairs are on paper only.

FRAUNCES
TAVERN

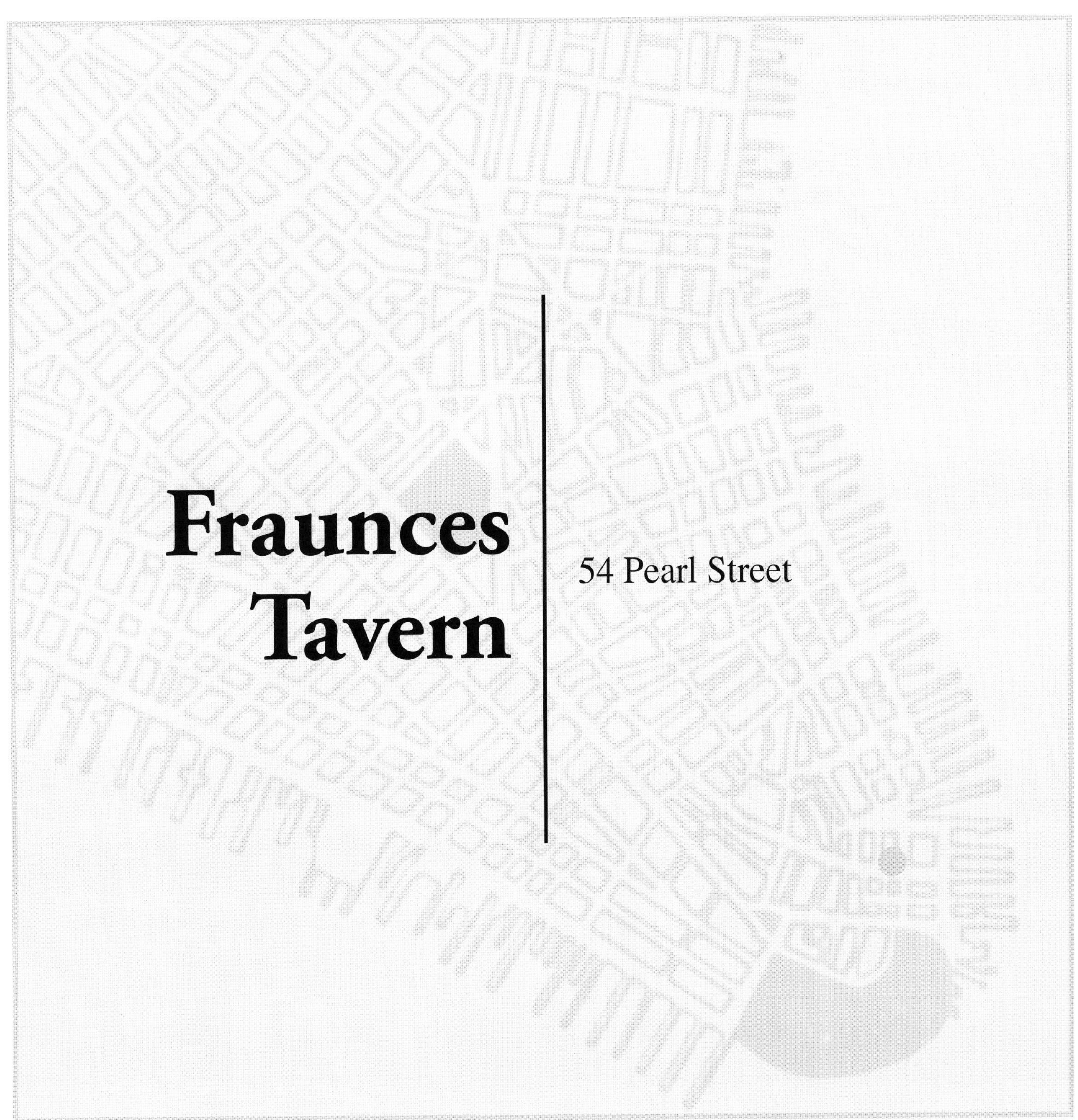

# Fraunces Tavern

54 Pearl Street

FRAUNCES TAVERN

*Even if you failed U.S. history, you will recognize the names and dates associated with the early years of Fraunces Tavern. 1775, 1776, 1783. Washington, Jefferson, Franklin, Hamilton.*

Like any group of power brokers, they needed a friendly spot to eat, drink, and network. Like any restaurant that rents out banquet rooms to the Chamber of Commerce, Fraunces Tavern rented its space to the power brokers we now call the Founding Fathers. And thanks to the networking they accomplished here, we get a day off on the Fourth of July.

But even before there was a United States of America, there was a New York City (or New Amsterdam). The story of Fraunces Tavern includes some pretty famous names from city history as well, starting in 1686, when the site of 54 Pearl Street was granted to Stephanus Van Cortlandt by Mayor Nicholas Bayard, and continuing to 1700, when Van Cortlandt gave the property (then used as a landfill) to his daughter Anne as a present upon her wedding to Etienne Delancey.

Not one to "look a gift garbage dump in the mouth," Delancey constructed a three-story residence on the land in 1719. The structure still stands and is the main building for the Fraunces Tavern Museum. Over the years the building was used by Henry Holt, John Jay, and Governor George Clinton.

It was in 1762 that Samuel Fraunces purchased the building and opened the Queen's Head Tavern (also known as the Sign of the Queen Charlotte.) More names, more dates: The New York Chamber of Commerce was founded here in 1768, and the Sons of Liberty planned the New York Tea Party here in 1774. The New York Provincial Congress met at the Tavern in 1776. After the Revolution, Fraunces sold the Tavern, and the location housed the Department of Foreign Affairs, under John Jay. Later, the Department of Treasury under Alexander Hamilton, and the Department of War, under Henry Knox, operated here. But Fraunces Tavern's greatest moment in history came when George Washington bid farewell to his officers in the Long Room on December 4th, 1783.

It's hard to imagine a bar today figuring so prominently in the legitimate operations of government. But the role of inns and pubs during the eighteenth century is highlighted in the story of Fraunces Tavern. In many towns and cities, these drinking houses were the first places people heard the news of the day. They served as meeting grounds so merchants could conduct business and also as places where political and social ideas could be exchanged. Considering the contributions of Fraunces Tavern to the Revolution, it's fitting that it served the new Republic during its first years. Alexander Hamilton drank here, ran the Department of the Treasury here, and founded the Bank of New York around the corner.

*Alexander Hamilton drank here, ran the Department of the Treasury here, and founded the Bank of New York around the corner.*

After the federal government moved to Washington, the Tavern became a boarding house, and later a saloon. Fires nearly destroyed the building several times, but it was always rebuilt and added onto. By the end of the nineteenth century the original structure had been renovated beyond recognition.

In 1904, the City of New York, looking forward but not back, decided to tear down Fraunces Tavern to build a parking lot, the City's first. Fortunately, the Sons of the Revolution in the State of New York stepped in. They bought the site and hired architect William Mersereau to oversee the restoration. His work on the project is still being critiqued by students of architecture today. The building is currently owned by the Sons of the Revolution in the State of New York, who operate the Museum and lease out the Tavern business to a group of owner/managers. Fraunces Tavern is still a vital part of its neighborhood and a living bit of history in New York City.

Fraunces Tavern closed in 1999 while the Sons of the Revolution sought bids to operate the Tavern. More than 40 groups vied for the chance, but Mike Rakusin, and his partners, Damon Testaverde, Vincent DeSimone, and Robert Gillings, won. A detailed renovation began, covering the good part of a year. An original fireplace and mahogany bar were restored, along with fixtures and chandeliers. The muralist Janet Hanchey was hired to restore a historic mural of 1717 New York City that appears in the 68-seat Bissell Room. (It was here that a terrorist attack took place in 1975. The FALN, a Puerto Rican nationalist group, set off a bomb in the restaurant during lunch. Five people were killed and 50 injured. If you look closely, you will see a crack from the explosion in the mural.)

Two and one-half million dollars later, the Tavern was set to reopen. Then September 11, 2001 erupted. Only ten blocks from the World Trade Center, the entire neighborhood was devastated. Fraunces Tavern's careful renovation needed a renovation, for the dust found its way in and covered everything inside. But Rakusin was determined. "We were the first business to reopen after 9/11," he claims proudly. On the day Fraunces finally reopened, October 11, 2001, CNN ran a banner all day announcing it. In that day's issue of the *New York Post*, columnist Steve Dunleavy wrote that Fraunces Tavern "officially reopens today as a symbol of pride, patriotism, of course, and yes, damn it, downright defiance." On Thanksgiving Day 2001, the place was packed, and according to Mike Rakusin, "We served 700 people that day." A lot of regulars, and visitors from over the years made sure to show their support for Fraunces Tavern, Lower Manhattan, and New York City.

Fraunces Tavern has worked its way into urban legends, mostly concerning various hauntings said to have occurred there. According to Fraunces Tavern Museum Curator Nadezhda Williams and Director Amy Adamo, these stories consist of sounds of parties going on in the rooms upstairs that were used as private party rooms centuries ago. Folks who work there during the off hours have seen and heard manifestations. During the year-long restoration, Security Guard Linsford Bennett routinely heard sounds. "As soon as I came upstairs, they stopped." he said. "It sounded like a group of men talking and laughing." Other workers have claimed to see a Continental soldier running from room to room or a woman walking along the upstairs landing. (Supposedly the woman is the ghost of Ballerina Anna Gardie, who was living in Fraunces Tavern in 1798 when it was a boarding house. She and her husband were found dead in an apparent murder-suicide.) But the ghosts haven't kept anyone from working or enjoying their time at Fraunces. If anything, the mystery adds to the history.

Fraunces Tavern has survived war, the British Occupation (7 years in Manhattan), several fires, almost being torn down for a parking lot, the FALN bombing, and 9/11. Their loyal customers, mostly a lunch crowd, include some of the richest and most powerful names on Wall Street. (Witness "Blaney's Corner," named after regular Jim Blaney, the biggest sugar trader in the world.) It's still a neighborhood bar. It's just that since this is the oldest neighborhood in New York, this is a very old bar. But the modern innovations on the menu and behind the bar fit right in. Just as in the (very) old days, the bankers and traders and politicos (City Hall is around the corner, don't forget) meet and drink and even sing here on occasion. Karaoke Thursdays are popular, and as Rakusin says with a characteristic grin, they may sing today's pop tunes but "it's our 'Yankee Doodle Dandy.'" Alexander Hamilton's original employees at the Bank of New York came here after work for a drink, and their counterparts two hundred years later are doing the same.

WARNING
WA'TER·MEL'ON

# J.G. Melon

1291 Third Avenue
at 74th Street

J.G.
MELON

*J.G. Melon opened exactly in the right place at exactly the right time, and has remained one of the most popular neighborhood bars in New York.*

Originally known as the Central Bar, which was built and owned by Rupert's Brewery, the place was a speakeasy during Prohibition. When it opened as J.G. Melon in 1972, the drinking age was 18, and the Upper East Side was thickly populated with tony prep schools–a combination that made attracting customers easy. J.G. Melon proved a fast favorite with prepsters armed with cash and a license to party. Then, when *New York* magazine reported that an interior designer had brought his wealthy clients there on a slumming expedition, the place became a hit with parents as well. Suddenly the mayor was drinking there, the governor was drinking there, and every Kennedy within a 50-mile radius was drinking there. Grace Kelly had to wait an hour for a table and sat at the bar drinking Heineken out of the bottle. In fact, so many famous faces turned up that they, who usually wait at no restaurant, had to wait for tables at a dinky little bar. There just weren't enough regular folks for the celebrities to jump ahead of. How did they all find out about J.G. Melon? Word of mouth, says longtime manager and partner Shaun Young. "I asked President and Mrs. Ford how they heard about our place when they came in, and the president said, 'I asked my friends where to go in New York for a hamburger, and they all told me J.G. Melon.'"

The ubiquitous Upper East Side bar, it has shown up in films and commercials, most notably in a scene from *Kramer vs. Kramer.* And located in the middle of the room is Steve's Table, named after writer Steve Gordon, who wrote his Oscar-nominated screenplay for *Arthur* at J.G. Melon. Shawn Young shakes his head, "He dropped dead just before the movie came out." Because Gordon was nice guy and a regular, Young and the staff keep the memorial preserved, along with several others at the bar. There are plaques and objects on the wall above the bar, with a regular's pipe, or tennis racket, or favorite seat marked. "Once," laughs Young, "a guy comes in here and sees the plaques, and he says to me, 'I'd like to get up on that wall. How do I do that?' and

I told him 'You don't want to be on the wall because that would mean you're dead.'"

Trendy bars come and trendy bars go, but J.G. Melon is one trendy nightspot that has simply stayed. It sailed through the eighties and nineties, hosting regulars such as Billy Martin, Brooke Shields, Andre Agassi, and Jerry Seinfeld and his then-girlfriend Shoshana Lonstein. Local celebrities loved the joint, too, like Viki Gotti, the Dapper Don's daughter, and her friend, beloved regular, the late Andy Capasso, who once sent Young a photo of his classic Buick with a melon on the hood. (The photo is over the bar, along with many melon pictures and sculptures that decorate the place.) One reason for J.G. Melon's staying power is the relaxed atmosphere. Another is the burger, argued to be among the three best in New York. (According to Bobby Flay, there is no contest. The burger at J.G. Melon is "the best in the city.") Protein addicts love the cheeseburgers and will put away several at one sitting. Says Young, "Bruce Cutler used to come in and eat four and five at a time."

*It sailed through the eighties and nineties, hosting regulars such as Billy Martin, Brooke Shields, Andre Agassi, and Jerry Seinfeld and his then-girlfriend Shoshana Lonstein.*

A third reason is the management's lack of interest in alerting the media about their wealthy and well-known clientele. According to Young, "We've never called Page Six. We've never had the press here to take pictures." And so you can sit at the bar and watch as the ladies-who-lunch scarf down burgers, Hermes scarves be damned. Their secret is safe with the other patrons and staff. And yes, darling, they *will* have fries with that.

Another big draw was J.G. Melon's celebrity bartender, actor Dylan McDermott's father, Mac McDermott. Mac had once owned the West 4th Street Saloon, where Dylan was a bartender before Hollywood whispered its siren song in his ear. When Mac sold his place he went to tend bar at Melon's. As Dylan's career took off, people began to show up at the bar simply because Mac was working there. He developed such a following that in August 2002, when he moved to Scottsdale, Page Six wrote about it, and the paper in Scottsdale had the story on the front page. About 400 people showed up at the going away party at J.G. Melon.

The preppies still party here. Some of the regulars came here in high school and today bring their kids in. The bar's famous Bloody Marys are still excellent, and the burgers and cottage fries are still flying off the grill. At dinner time there's usually a line out the door. Seems like J.G. Melon is here to stay. Which makes thousands of New Yorkers—and Bobby Flay—very happy.

Tanqueray
IMPORTED
BOMBAY
DRY GIN
1761
GORDON'S
DRY GIN
STOCK
VERMOUTH
EXTRA DRY
SMIRNOFF
FINLANDIA
STOLICHNAYA
RUSSIAN VODKA
ABSOLUT
CITRON
ABSOLUT
IMPORTED
Ketel One
VODKA
Imported
Dewar's
White Label
MYERS'S
RUM
Seagram's
7
OLD
GRAND-DAD
WHISKEY
Maker's
Mark
JAMESON
GONE

Miss Keens
CHOPHOUSE
Keens
Ale
AMSTEL
light

# Keens Steakhouse

72 West 36$^{th}$ Street

Bank
72
Keens
STEAKHOUSE
KEENS CHOPHOUSE
SPRINKLER SHUT OFF
VALVE DIRECTLY BELOW

*In 1977, historic Keens Steakhouse, a Herald Square landmark, was on the brink of demolition. Locals and regulars, as well as longtime employees, were truly depressed. Keens wasn't just a restaurant. It had history, a real history.*

But Keens was dead, or about to be. The last chop was flame-broiled and served, the last pipe was smoked, and though no priest came to read the Last Rites, a reporter from the *New York Times* wrote about its passing. For it must pass. How could it be saved? Who could take on the hundred-year-old building, and its business, and repair it and make a go of it, during one of the worst economic crises New York has ever known?

When all else fails, call in the artists. They are the only ones with the imagination and vision, along with the practical skills, to pull it off. It doesn't hurt if it's an artist with some money, either.

A doctor and restaurateur, George Schwarz, and his wife, the late artist Kiki Kogelnik, fresh from their success at One Fifth in the Village, entered to save the day. Kogelnik and Schwarz, rushing in where no sensible angel has any business, took on the challenge. They bought the old place and lovingly refurbished it, retaining every nook and cranny and everything in them. Thanks to these folks, New York still has one of its most unique bars, restored and bustling for more than 20 years.

Keens was founded in 1885 by one Albert Keen, a well-known theatrical producer in what was then the Theater District in New York, Herald Square. The second floor of the restaurant housed the Lambs Club, a branch of the original theatrical and literary club in London. Keens Chophouse (as it was called at that time) soon became a favorite with actors and players in New York theater, and it was common to see actors in full makeup and costumes dash in from the Garrick Theater, which abutted Keens back-to-back, for a quick drink between acts. Producers, playwrights, publishers, and journalists (the *New York Herald* was on the Square) all crowded into the men-only bar and pipe room for a pewter mug of ale or a smoke, or both. This, plus the favored offering of two pound mutton chops, made Keens a Victorian man's dream.

This dream was shattered, of course, by a Victorian woman, none less than actress Lillie Langtry, who swept into Keens in 1901 and had to sue the restaurant to get her mutton chop. Keens recovered gracefully, mounting a sign that read, "Ladies are in luck, they can dine at Keens." Now women were free to don their dresses with leg o'mutton sleeves and eat…mutton. They seemed happy enough, and as the years went on, customers of both sexes continued to patronize the place. In 1935, the one millionth mutton chop was sold, amid fanfare and mint sauce.

Albert Keen opened a Pipe Club as part of Lambs and continued the club when he opened Keens. With a lifetime membership for five dollars, a member would keep his pipe (or hers) at the club. The reason for the club stems as much from tradition as it does from practicality. In England, clay pipes, or "churchwardens" as they were called, were preferred. These pipes were too fragile to carry from place to place, and so the custom of leaving them at one's tavern or club became popular practice. Keens modeled itself on this old tradition, and had a pipe warden, who catalogued the collection, and pipe boys who delivered the pipes tableside. Numbered and stored hanging from the rafters, the pipes today, some 50,000 of them, started out their lives made of white porous clay, but are now brown with age and smoke. The ones with broken stems are those belonging to the faithful departed.

*Keens modeled itself on this old tradition, and had a pipe warden, who catalogued the collection, and pipe boys who delivered the pipes tableside.*

But back to Kiki and George, who came on the scene relatively late in Keens's life. Initially told that it would cost about $30,000 to renovate the place, they forged ahead. Ahead into a restoration that ended up taking more than three years and costing more than $1.4 million. When you have 50,000 pipes to take down gingerly before you can install an updated air conditioning system, it costs money. Nobody could stand in the cellar, so the ceiling needed to be raised. The bar was too short and it needed lengthening, and during its removal, the floor was discovered to be dangerously sagging. In the end it was worth every penny. Every artifact was cleaned and restored.

There are a lot of artifacts here. Drinking at Keens is like drinking in a museum, only you can go up close to the exhibits. There are more than 500 pieces of theatrical memorabilia, postcards and playbills from more than a hundred years ago. Most precious among these is a playbill from *Our American Cousin* that is purportedly the one that Lincoln was holding when he was shot. There are brown stains on the playbill, supposedly Lincoln's blood. A newspaper clipping from the era is framed on the wall and tells the story of how the playbill was retrieved from under Lincoln's seat after the assassination, and how it ended up at Keens. The Smithsonian may be very interested to examine this playbill closely, but for now, it's on display in Keens's Lincoln Room.

*There are brown stains on the playbill, supposedly Lincoln's blood.*

There's a huge painting by Alexander Pope and a lithograph billboard for *Peck's Bad Boy*. There are nineteenth century political cartoons from *Puck* and *Punch* in the Lincoln Room. There are photos of the Shakespearean actors who formed the original Lambs Club in London and a Mason & Hamlin grand piano. There is a room devoted to Keens regular Teddy Roosevelt, that old Knickerbocker, with Bull Moose Party and Rough Rider memorabilia. There's an authentic British Royal Coat of Arms, carved in oak, that came from Hearst Castle. There are pipes, lots and lots of pipes, everywhere you look. The ones owned by famous people are kept in display cases in the foyer. Buffalo Bill, Herbert Hoover, Babe Ruth, General MacArthur, Adlai Stevenson, Will Rogers, Florenz Ziegfeld, Albert Einstein, and practically every mayor since the turn of the last century are represented.

The food at Keens has remained true to its history. Now a chop and steak house, Keens continues to enjoy a loyal following. The theaters may have moved uptown long ago, but Madison Square Garden and midtown are just a couple of blocks away. The pipe smokers are gone, though once in a while someone comes in to claim a pipe. Manager Bonnie Jenkins, who's been with Schwarz for fifteen years, says that recently a woman came in for her grandfather's pipe. It took a bit of doing to track it down. (There are 90,000 of them, after all.) "We were on chairs with the flashlights, peering at numbers," says Jenkins good-naturedly. They found it, and the inheritor brought it home to proudly display. Is it hard keeping watch over so many objects, so much history? Jenkins smiles. She clearly loves her job. "There are times when I ask Kiki (who died in 1997) for help," she says. Kogelnik put so much creative and hands-on energy into Keens, it became a labor of love for the artist, and her mark is still there more than 20 years later. Thanks to her, an Austrian-born citizen, and Schwarz, who was born in Frankfurt and escaped the Nazis as a child, New York has preserved some key moments in its own, and the nation's, history.

72

# King Cole Bar

2 East 55th Street
At the St. Regis Hotel

OLD KING COLE

*Gliding into the foyer of The St. Regis, you can see not only how the other half lives, but how gorgeous and relaxing that life really is. Crystal chandeliers, thick carpets, polished marble, and a highly attentive staff lull you into a sense of serenity.*

Settle into a cozy leather chair or banquette in the King Cole Bar, and you are ready for even more soothing. The bartender looks genuinely happy to see you. You may be one of New York's or Hollywood's power brokers, the kind that end up leaving a great big tip. Or you may be of simpler means, out to savor the best that New York has to offer. Either way, the bar staff is ready to serve you in a way that only hotel bars can. If The St. Regis is the Queen of all New York hotels, the King Cole Bar is her king, and you are the noble guest.

The St. Regis Hotel was built in 1904 by one of America's royals, Colonel John Jacob Astor IV, who eight years later became the Titanic's most famous victim. The Colonel spent $5.5 million to construct the hotel and furnish it. Operating on the concept of "if you build it, they will come," he opened one of the great hotels of the world, and it was soon filled with the social elites that formed the "400," the social group created by Colonel Astor's mother. The King Cole Bar was the ultimate gentleman's club, furnished in rich wood and leather, the easier to keep clean when the cigars left their residue. it was a gentleman's club in the literal sense: women were barred until 1950. Though the stuffy atmosphere has dissipated, it has retained that private men's club feel, and for years was one of the great cigar bars in New York, until the new smoking restrictions left the bar's two state-of-the-art humidors lying fallow.

In 1932, the famous mural by Maxwell Parrish was removed from the Astor's Knickerbocker Hotel and reinstalled in the King Cole Bar. A sign above the doorway in Latin was added with the whimsical quote: "I'd like to die in a tavern and be given a sip of wine. Then I could sing happily with the angels, 'May God be kind to the drinker!'" Adding to the jocularity, there is a secret code of sorts in the picture, and the discerning viewer can probably figure it out just by studying the expressions on each figure's face. If you get stuck, the bartender will be glad to tell you. If you still don't get it, here it is in writing: King Cole was not only a merry old soul but a flatulent one as well. So much for the dignity of royalty.

During Prohibition, regulars in this exclusive enclave would arrive with their favorite bottle or flask and buy mixers to make their drinks with. Bartenders also kept secret stashes under lock and key for their best patrons, using a variety of hiding places. (In many wood paneled bars, individual panels served as safes. The Union Club turned its paneling into lockers, with each member having his own key.) With tactics like these, the King Cole Bar sailed through Prohibition with little effect. In 1934, St. Regis bartender Fernand Petiot introduced a cocktail called the Red Snapper, which was soon renamed the Bloody Mary. Though at The King Cole Bar they retained the original name, as it was felt that "Bloody Mary" was too vulgar.

*The Union Club turned its paneling into lockers, with each member having his own key.*

Since its founding, The St. Regis was home for personalities and icons, as well as the quietly rich. Colonel Serge Obolensky, the Russian Prince who escaped the Revolution and later married Alice Astor; Michael Arlen, the novelist; Marlene Dietrich; William Paley and his wife Barbara ("Babe") all lived at The St. Regis, as did Salvador Dali and his wife Gala. Actress Gertrude Lawrence instructed her agent to arrange all her press appointments at The St. Regis. Today, The St. Regis is still a popular site for press junkets and interviews for Hollywood elite.

Bartender Gavin Fitzgibbon stands at the ready to provide some of that famous royal treatment. Like a courtier, he knows that the art of conversation is key to success. "It's all about conversation and social lubrication," says Fitzgibbon. In a place like King Cole, a little effort can go a long way. Let's just say there are a lot of rich people around. "Naturally generous or stupid money," grins Fitzgibbon. "I get guys in here–captains of industry–they could squash a guy like me for lunch." One of his favorite games is guessing who's on the other end of the cell phone. These are the guys who drop $190 for a shot of Remy Martin Louis XIII or $325 for a bottle of Dom Perignon—and what the hell, buy a round for the house. It's not unusual for them to run up a $4,000-$5,000 tab. Gavin Fitzgibbon's best tip? Back in the flush 90s, $1,200 on a $100 tab. The customer? Name forgotten but, "He'd just sold his company to Microsoft," he remembers.

Today, there are still enough stars and money floating around King Cole Bar to keep everyone happy. Pierce Brosnan, Sean Penn, Demi Moore, not to mention practically every agent from CAA and William Morris. When Demi Moore came for her last stay, it was at the height of the Ashton Kutcher splash. Fitzgibbon recounts that suddenly "every manager from the upstairs offices were very interested in coming down to the bar to commend me for the great job I do." Trouble was, they barely looked at him while they gave him kudos, their eyes locked and loaded on Demi. Then there are the after parties, like the one after the Tony Awards. "Nathan Lane, Victor Garber, Martin Short. They all came in and started singing and dancing–it was great!" It's fun to work in such a place, notes Fitzgibbon. Nice work, if you can get it.

If you can't afford $190 for a shot of Remy, here's the recipe for the famous Red Snapper. (Even working joes and janes deserve a little royal treatment.)

## *Red Snapper from King Cole Bar*

1 1/2 oz. vodka
6-8 oz. Sacramento tomato juice
white pepper
black pepper
celery salt
lemon juice

In a glass with ice, combine vodka and tomato juice. Add spices to taste. Stir and enjoy, preferably on a Sunday morning, with eggs, bacon, toast, and *The New York Times.*

W. H. AUDEN
A Biography
JIM ROHWER
ASIA RISING
WILL DURANT
THE AGE OF FAITH

# The Library

540 Park Avenue
The Regency Hotel

LITTLE WOMEN
MAY ALCOTT
NOT WITHOUT
LANGSTON HUGHES
ASIA RISING

*Elegant, comfortable, and built for the fast crowd, The Library at The Regency is the Lexus of hotel bars.*

From the moment the doors open for the famous Power Breakfast to the late night cabaret hosted by Michael Feinstein, this bar is a lot like the high-octane executives it serves—it never seems to sleep but always manages to look great and perform superbly.

The Tisch family, owners of Loews Hotels, opened The Regency in 1964. The hotel quickly became a clubhouse for sports figures and celebrities. They drank at the bar, and then repaired upstairs to their reserved rooms and suites. Mickey Mantle practically lived here, and the Rat Pack and their hard-drinking cronies bent their expensively-tailored elbows here, too. Back in the party-hearty 60s and 70s, it was the kind of place where the regulars would slip the maitre d' $50 to hold a table for them, "just in case,"—in case they met a certain someone they'd like to get to know better. It evolved into a reservations-only spot. The system worked great for the regulars, not so great for anyone else. "It was like a men's club here," says restaurant manager Rae Bianco, who's been at The Library since 1995. "The regulars had their tables, but if anyone else came in, it felt cliquey." The Regency began to lose customers and some of its luster. The bar began to attract prostitutes. (Hey, it's what happens when you have liquor, beds, and men in the same building.) But there was no doubt that it was time for a change.

Enter Jonathan Tisch. In 1995, he decided to close The Regency, renovate, and reopen. Total facelift, top to bottom. He use only the best designers and architects. He gently but firmly swept out the table-hogging regulars and their lady friends. "He looked around the room and said, 'It's time for the hookers to retire,'" laughs Bianco. While it's not known if any of them had pension plans, what is known is that the change proved an immediate success. No more reservations meant anyone could come in and have a table in the bar. The refurbished bar, renamed The Library, was designed by David Rockwell and had morphed into what its name indicates: a book nook that old-timers and newcomers applauded. What was missing, though, was the bar. And the bartender. At least visibly, that is.

In a revolution of sorts, Rockwell and Tisch took out the bar at The Regency. It is serviced by the same bartender, Gene McAnuff, who's been there since The Regency opened in 1964. Only now instead of serving customers face-to-face, trading news, jokes, and politics with them, he makes drinks in the kitchen, at a service bar. Essentially, your drinks are butlered to you in The Library, which is really more like a lounge than a true bar. While some people didn't notice the change, the regulars were outraged. Says McAnuff, "I had some customers who screamed in the lobby," they were so angry at McAnuff's banishment to the back. You can't blame them for being upset. After all, McAnuff was a good bartender, who understood about building relationships. He explains, "Bartending's not just drink making...a good bartender listens...because people need someone neutral to bare their soul to." Thirty years behind the bar added up to thousands of heart to heart conversations. The regulars missed their bartender, some still send him holiday cards, though the bar was removed in 1995.

*Only now instead of serving customers face-to-face, trading news, jokes, and politics with them, he makes drinks in the kitchen, at a service bar.*

But McAnuff is philosophical about it all. He misses the contact, of course, but he had plenty of that for years. The place was packed every night. "In the old days, people drank more. They'd have two martini lunches, then back to work, then out for more drinks after work, and then out to dinner. If someone didn't drink, they'd be regarded with some suspicion…how could you trust someone who doesn't drink?"

And drink at The Regency, they did: Elizabeth Taylor and Richard Burton (who once checked in at the same time Eddie Fisher was checking out), Mickey Mantle, Billy Martin. When Sinatra came in, he stayed 'til he was ferreted out by other customers and had to leave, just as occurred on one quiet Sunday afternoon when the wedding party in the next room discovered Ol' Blue Eyes was in the bar. According to McAnuff, "The next thing you know, the whole wedding came in here. Poor Frank! He just got his check and got out as fast as he could."

His best tipper? It's a toss-up between Billy Martin and Mickey Mantle. But Mantle wins as best customer. In fact, he would have been better had McAnuff not had to cut him off on several occasions. He says, "I used to tell his manager, 'I don't want to be the bartender that killed Mickey Mantle.'" McAnuff remembers Billy Martin most fondly. They had lots of talks, some of them the soul-baring kind. Martin, who had a terrible reputation with the press, came to depend on McAnuff to shield him from press-unfriendly situations at The Regency. They used a set of signals, not unlike those that a pitcher and catcher use. "When Billy'd come in, he'd look over at me, and if it was good at the bar, I'd give him the sign, and if it was bad I'd point to the restaurant, to the tables." When the coast cleared, Martin would make his way to McAnuff's bar. That kind of bartender/customer relationship is what McAnuff misses most. But while the echoes of clinking glasses and laughter may have faded, their memory still brings a twinkle to McAnuff's eye. They were pretty good old days, after all.

Today, The Library is used in the mornings for the legendary Power Breakfasts, so full of movers and shakers that Bianco says, "My jaw drops every day at who walks in this door." A typical customer list may include such political and business luminaries as Rudy Giuliani, Rev. Al Sharpton, Howard Dean, Robert Kennedy, Jr., David Dinkins, William Rudin, Edward Stern, and Keisha Sutton. Founded almost 30 years ago by Bob and Jon Tisch, the Founders Circle includes former New York mayors John Lindsay, Abe Beame, Ed Koch, and David Dinkins, and former Governor Hugh Carey, as well as *New York* magazine restaurant critic Gael Greene and chairman of Inner City Broadcasting, Percy Sutton. A fair amount of decisions affecting New York City have been made at a Regency Power Breakfast, right in The Library. Forget about if walls could talk, what walls need to do at a Power Breakfast is listen and take notes.

The Library is the place where guests of The Regency will stop in for a drink, whether it's members of the Knicks, (who stay at the hotel when they're playing at the Garden), or celebs stopping in at Feinstein's, The Library can get really star-studded. Run by cabaret legend Michael Feinstein, every night the restaurant becomes a nightclub in the old New York tradition: fine service and great entertainment, along with some fantastic people-watching. When Carole Bayer Sager played here, Carly Simon, Carole King, Bette Midler, Hugh Jackman, and Burt Bacharach all came in on the same night. Between Feinstein's friends and the acts he books, the crowd is as good as the show. So at The Library, everything old is new again, or as Carly Simon once wrote, "These are the good old days."

*When Carole Bayer Sager played here, Carly Simon, Carole King, Bette Midler, Hugh Jackman, and Burt Bacharach all came in on the same night.*

Marion's
CONTINENTAL

# Marion's Continental Restaurant & Lounge

354 Bowery

YCO INC
352 BOWERY
MARION'S
CONTINENTAL
Restaurant & Lounge
595-3

*With a history that features an international beauty, Iron-Curtain intrigue, the glamorous nightclub scene of the 1950s, and a successful comeback by the founder's son—what doesn't the Marion's Continental story have?*

It all began in post-war Hungary, when young (her exact age unknown, even by her children) Marion Nagy conceived a plan to escape to the West. As a member of the Hungarian Swim Team, Marion was invited to participate in the Peace Games in Paris. It was the perfect opportunity and Marion took it, traveling to France and to freedom.

She didn't speak French, but she had beauty and poise beyond her years, so she used them to her best advantage and became a model. Not just any model either, but a high-fashion model, in the best couture houses in France. Her exotic looks put her in high demand on the runways and in the salons, and she found herself becoming rather famous. But fame had its dangers during the Cold War, when successful defectors would sometimes meet with untimely ends. So, as she became well-known, Marion sensed that all was not well. In 1950, she decided to leave the Continent altogether. She crossed the pond, as a fashion model should, in style on the Queen Elizabeth and set up her new life in New York.

Marion's arrival in post-War New York couldn't have been better timed. The city was jammed with people starting over, and nightclubs and parties were abundant. Marion resumed her modeling career and established herself as a hostess, throwing such legendary parties that people urged her to open a place of her own. With a French chef, Jean-Claude, she found a small storefront down on the Bowery and opened Marion's Continental Restaurant and Lounge. By her son's best guess, she was 22 years old.

Before Rolodexes, people had friends, and Marion had a long list of them, important ones, too. Soldiers, statesmen, presidents, entertainers—all the glitterati. These were the hard-drinking Fifties, and the ability to hold both one's liquor and a witty conversation were the two most important social skills of the

day. Places like Marion's Continental were a necessity to keep those skills sharp. The drinks were great, the food and service excellent, and the crowd deluxe: Marion's Continental became the must-visit spot downtown.

Marion presided over it all, seeing to the details and enjoying the attentions of some famous suitors, including Richard Burton and Rex Harrison. Celebrity guests were asked to sign a dinner plate; patrons from the old days may remember seeing them on display. Along with the photographs, they are a record of the famous names and faces that peopled New York at the time.

In 1973, Marion closed the lounge. She had married and had had three children by then, and she left the business to raise her family in Belmar, New Jersey. So the story ends, until 1990.

In 1990, one of her sons, Richard Bach, decided to reopen his mom's place. Unfortunately Marion had passed away, having lived to see all three of her children go into the restaurant business. The building was available, though it had been reconverted to a storefront. The idea came to Bach, and he liked it. He bought the place, and using old photos, he reconstructed Marion's Continental.

Sometimes comebacks fall flat, but this one had a legacy to move it forward. Like the original, it was a hit and attracted celebrities and the party elite. They came for the nightclub ambiance and the playful campiness of the place. They stayed for the relaxed atmosphere and the no-paparazzi rule. So we don't have any pictures of Madonna and her then-"porn boyfriend" cavorting and almost consorting at their table one night.

Like his mom did, Bach gives his guests the room to play and presides over it all, over the glamorous, the up-and-coming, and the regulars. Discretion is necessary in handling them all, whether famous and drunk, or romantic and drunk, or famous, romantic and drunk. The bathroom has become a love nest on several occasions. Bach smiles just a little as he explains, "The sink has been replaced four times."

Like Marion, he pays attention to the details. His staff has custom-designed uniforms each season. The service is excellent, his bar staff limited to a certain number of shifts per week, "so they don't get burnt out." The bartenders of Marion's Continental created the Metropolitan, and one of them wrote a book about her experience tending bar here. (Ty Wenzel, *Behind Bars*). And they show uncommon dedication to their regulars—so much so, that the New York Press, which sponsors the "Best of" Awards, gave them the award for "Best Reasons to Be Asked to Leave a Bar" because of their particular care for one of their patrons, a public relations guy named Frank.

Throughout the 90s, Frank was a regular. He sat at the same stool at the bar, and this being the days before almost everyone carried a cell phone, used the pay phone a lot. Marion's Continental was sort of his office. When he'd be on the phone for an extended period, some patron would invariably try to grab his seat, but the bartenders always defended it with "Sorry, that's Frank's chair." Any resistance was met with that customer being asked to leave. And so "It's Frank's chair" became the "Best Reason to Be Asked to Leave a Bar." And you thought that kind of dedicated service went down with the Titanic!

> *And so "It's Frank's chair" became the "Best Reason to Be Asked to Leave a Bar."*

These days, Bach has expanded the business to include a catering service, a burlesque hall called The Marquee, and a reconstruction of the nineteenth century gay bar called The Slide. There are all kinds of themed parties here, including fashion brunches, a sort of fitting tribute to Marion and her beginnings. Yet while Marion's spirit is present, it's a happy haunting and not an overbearing one. Bach has managed to retain the essence of the original establishment while improvising and improving along the way. Marion would be proud.

ny
BUDLIGHT
PETER McMANUS

# Peter McManus Cafe

152 Seventh Avenue
at 19th Street

ZAGAT
RATED

*Jamo McManus may very well be the friendliest man in all of New York City. Nobody has a bad word to say about him.*

Not his customers, some of them regulars since the days when his Dad, James Sr., owned the place. Not his competitors. (That says a lot.) Not his staff, some of whom have worked here for more than 20 years. (That says even more.) He's that kind of guy; down-to-earth, easygoing, and generous. The result is the kind of friendly place "where everybody knows your name," that imitators imitate but never quite get right. In fact, when Cheers went off the air, a local paper suggested that viewers visit Peter McManus Cafe as a replacement. When you're here, you're part of the family.

Places like McManus's are all but gone from New York, and with them, a way of life best described as "neighborhood." Jamo McManus learned about neighborhood from his dad, James McManus, Sr., who inherited "The Store" (his mother thought that sounded nicer than "the bar") from his father, founder Peter McManus. First opened in 1911 on the East Side, Peter McManus Cafe has been in Chelsea since 1936 and is the oldest family-run bar in Manhattan. The cafe sits where there used to be a bakery and a drug store. The year 1936 might not sound like so long ago, until Jamo remarks that the renovation in 1936 cost $30,000. It was a time when the bar menu featured a ham sandwich for 25 cents and chicken-and-two-vegetables for 80 cents. Suddenly, 1936 seems a very long time ago. And throughout its tenure, McManus Cafe has provided countless regular guys and gals with a place to come after work to knock back a few, watch the game or the races, and have a bit of chat. "We are the poor man's country club," smiles Jamo McManus.

The place has become a neighborhood fixture, with first James Sr., and later, Jamo, at the helm. Always in a shirt and tie, always serving a reasonably-priced drink and offering simple food for a good price. A real Irish bar, "not an imitation old-time one," says Jamo. The wooden bar is an old beauty, 75 feet long, with seven types of wood in its heavily carved back. There's Tiffany glass in the doors and back bar, and between that and the atmosphere, it's no surprise that the Cafe has been used several times in movies, most notably *Radio Days*, *Highlander*, and *Keeping the Faith*. *Seinfeld* and *Law & Order* shot scenes here, too.

McManus Sr., who died in 2001, was a legend. He cared about Chelsea when nobody cared about Chelsea, running the first Chelsea Clean Up program using free beer as an incentive. A brilliant idea, that. He was especially famous for his Stingers. One night Yankees Mel Allen and the original "M & M," Mantle and Maris, came in for some serious drinking. James Sr. made a batch of his Stingers, and fourteen drinks later, Mel Allen "had to be poured into the back of his fancy convertible," Jamo laughs.

*One night Yankees Mel Allen and the original "M & M," Mantle and Maris, came in for some serious drinking.*

James McManus, Sr. knew that it was the little things that made the world go 'round. During the Blackouts of 1965 and 1979, he gave away milk to the mothers in the neighborhood and bent the law by staying open way past closing (claiming he couldn't tell the time because the clocks had stopped). Beloved in Chelsea, he also oversaw that bastion of New York City athletics, the stickball game. Stickball games invariably closed down 19th Street and brought together the whole neighborhood. On those days the beer would flow and James Sr. would be in his element. These were his people. "This was Dad's second family," his son Brian told the *Irish Voice*, "[This place] meant everything to him."

Consider Bruce the Bartender, who, before he was hired, lost his apartment and all his possessions in a fire. "Give him a check," McManus Sr. told his son. "For how much?" Jamo asked. "Leave it blank," he was told. "He can fill it in himself." That's the kind of man McManus was. The guy was so well loved that when he died, *The New York Times* included a quarter-page obituary with a picture. And then there were the *Saturday Night Live* skits featuring Chris Farley's character Jack McManus, the friendly Irish bartender, who was based on James Sr. You *know* you're an institution when SNL imitates you. That beats a big spread in the obit section, even if it *is* the *Times*.

Friendly Irish bartender he was, but make no mistake, McManus was no pushover. Twice awarded the Purple Heart during World War II, he survived a shooting during a robbery in the 70s. The bullet hole is still visible in a glass pane on the back bar. James Sr. learned the bar business working alongside his dad. Peter McManus gave James Sr. his first job during Prohibition, when Joe Kennedy's bootleggers would deliver booze to the McManus home in Far Rockaway. James Sr.'s job was to tap on the bottles and barrels and make sure they were full—not bad for a kid. In the back room of the Cafe there's a picture from the 1930s of some family and friends, one of Dutch Schultz's bodyguards among them. (Dutch was a McManus regular.)

McManus regulars are a hard-working bunch who like to watch the game, and bet on it. Overall, they are friendly to newcomers; still, they have not been above tossing someone out feet first when they don't like him. (Burt Reynolds was escorted thusly when, during the height of the Vietnam War, he made an anti-war comment at the bar.) The regulars are comfortable here, year in, year out. So comfortable, in fact, that they wouldn't leave even when the place was on fire. In 1975, an apartment upstairs caught fire, burning out the whole second story and causing a tenant's death, but the regulars in the bar downstairs refused to get out. The firefighters were arriving before some of them finally left—carrying their drinks with them, of course.

St. Patrick's Day is the biggest day of the year at McManus. Jamo's son, Justin, used to come in dressed like a leprechaun when he was a kid. When he got older, he tended bar. The experience didn't hurt him any. Justin attended Cornell, and since graduation has gone on to work at one of the city's top restaurants as bar manager. Fourth generation of a pub-keeping family, he knows just about everyone in the industry in New York. One day he will take over for Jamo, but for now, his dad still runs the show. Just like his dad before him, Jamo keeps an eye on The Store till it's time for his son to take charge. "My father used to say 'Get out from behind that bar or I'll break your legs,'" remembers Jamo McManus. "Then it was, 'Get to work or I'll break your legs.'"

McManus regulars practically live here, but have any ever died here? Jamo pauses, because with such a long and colorful history, there have been more than one. But one stands out the most. A regular named Vinnie. A nice guy, Vinnie. Jamo goes on, "He had a glass eye. And one day he was sitting there and suddenly he slumped over. I thought that the stool had broken, and I reached over and grabbed him, but then I realized he had fallen off his stool, and then when I looked in his eyes, they both looked like glass eyes."

He pauses again, remembering Vinnie, gone but not forgotten by his second family at Peter McManus Cafe. Justin, who at the time was head altar boy at St. Patrick's Cathedral, served at Vinnie's funeral Mass. Now *that's* neighborhood.

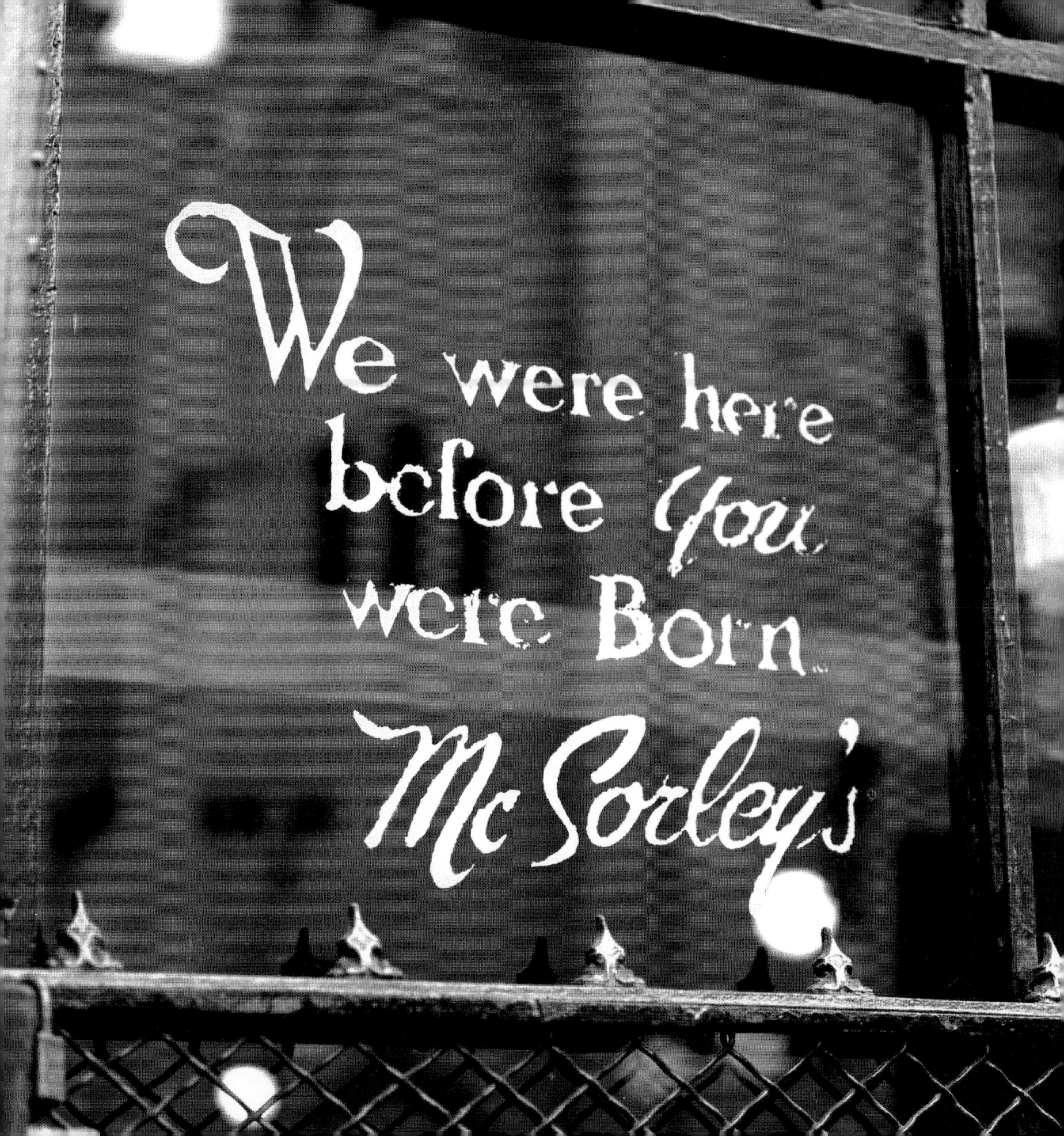

We were here before You were Born.
McSorley's

# McSorley's Old Ale House

15 East Seventh Street

Geoffrey
Bartholomew
14211
No Smoking

## *"Be good or be gone," reads the sign in McSorley's back room, and according to bartender Steven "Pepe" Zwaryczuk, it's a motto they live by.*

Though they haven't had to test it—much. Most McSorley's customers love the old place so much they won't stir up trouble here, and any newcomers are so in awe of its history, which even the sawdust on the floor seems soaked in, that they tend to drink quietly. But it isn't always that way, and it hasn't always been that way. There are nights when young men still come to test their endurance in this bastion of Irish male drinking culture. Suddenly the crowd can get a little rowdy. On such an occasion, Pepe merely has to point to the sign, and that, plus a better look at some of the stalwart regulars who would defend McSorley's like their own mother, is usually enough to ensure that any undesirables are either good, or gone. It's a system that's worked in one way or another since 1854.

That was the year John McSorley opened his pub, not long ago enough to say that Washington slept here, but long ago enough to say that Lincoln drank here. And if you believe McSorley's lore, Lincoln did stop in when he was in New York City in 1860. Although that is not *his* chair mounted over the bar, as legend often has it. The chair belonged to Peter Cooper, founder of The Cooper Union for the Advancement of Science and Art. A great good friend of John McSorley and a devoted regular to the bar, Cooper hosted Lincoln at Cooper Union, where the young lawyer made the speech that catapulted him from obscurity into the White House. Lincoln's visit to McSorley's has never been documented, but given that the school is steps away from the bar, and the night had brought freezing rain and snow, it seems very likely the stories are true that Lincoln sought some warmth at John McSorley's potbellied stove. Whether Lincoln ever did set foot in McSorley's or not, the wanted poster for his assassin is original, displayed on a wall.

Lincoln may or may not have come here, but Teddy Roosevelt did for sure, although not when he was president. His visits are documented, including his signature in the guest book, which was stolen back in the forties. Scores of politicians, famous and scandalous, including, of course, JFK, drank here. Famous men are all well and good, or they're all well and gone, but the greatest thing about McSorley's is its regular customers. A startling mix of men, their descriptions read like a line from the song "That's Life"—fighters, poets, pawns, and kings.

It's the regular customers—the fighters, poets, and pawns, much more so than the kings—that have kept McSorley's heart pumping in its 150 years. As owner Matt Maher says, "The most important thing in a bar is people." This saying is more true at McSorley's than perhaps at any other bar in New York. At McSorley's, the regulars figure prominently in both its history and current life. And not just today's regulars either; there's such a loyalty among the McSorley's staff and patrons that both the living and deceased share equal importance. "Regular" status is difficult to earn, according to Bill Wander, McSorley's in-house historian. You have to be a patron for 30 years before you can call yourself a regular. But it's worth it, for when you're a regular here, you're a regular forever. They'll be talking about you for the next hundred years.

*That flask behind the bar? Oh, that holds the ashes of Bobby Bowles.*

That flask behind the bar? Oh, that holds the ashes of Bobby Bowles. Bobby was an artist and an ironworker who combined his talents and used salvaged wrought iron to create sculptures. When he died, he had his ashes put into his flask, which was engraved with the motto "Rusty Iron," and kept behind the bar in perpetuity. Which, when you're talking McSorley's, is the real deal. Bobby won't be moved. Ever. That's loyalty. Those impossibly dusty wishbones hanging over the bar? Those are the wishbones from the going-away dinners of doughboys who never returned from the Great War. Never dusted, never touched, the wishbones ensure that a part of these soldiers' lives will be remembered and their sacrifice appreciated, even while their own bones may lie in forgotten graves.

Today's regulars or bartenders will regale each other with stories of those colleagues from the past, with a freshness of memory that is unusual in this short-attention-span culture. This is a friendly haunting, and nobody is getting exorcised. These ghosts are the characters who, for a century and a half, gave this place a richness and depth that few bars have, and that very few bars can sustain for so long. This, plus McSorley's success in preserving its own traditions while running a very successful business, have secured for its landmark status. There really is no other place like it in the world.

Where else can a man say "give me a light" to the bartender and receive not a match, but two eight-ounce glasses of McSorley's own light ale? Not only is the language used a little differently here, but the arithmetic is off as well, for here "one and one" doesn't equal two, but sixteen—for it's one eight-ounce glass and one eight-ounce glass that makes a sixteen-ounce pint. Since the glass sizes are smaller, a McSorley's bartender will automatically give you a pair of glasses if you order a light ale or a dark porter, which are the only alcoholic beverages served here. You have to ask for only one glass if that's what you're wanting, and it costs more than half of a pair. But you wouldn't want only one glass. Hardly anyone does, though there *is* the story of one customer who complained to now-retired bartender Tommy Lloyd about receiving two glasses at once. "I only want one at a time," he said, and

McSORLEY'S OLD ALE HOUSE
ESTABLISHED 1854
15
This Is Our 150 Year And Ale Is Well
We were here before you were Born McSorley's
McSorley's Old Ale House And
McSorley's Established 1854
Owned And Operated By The Maher Family
No Smoking
No Smoking
McSORLEY'S
McSORLEY'S of NEW YORK
McSORLEY'S of NEW YORK

Tommy asked him why. "Because one always gets warm," came the answer. "Which one?" asked Tommy. The man pointed to one of the glasses. "Drink that one first," said Tommy Lloyd.

What other place is as beloved as McSorley's and has hosted, to quote Bill Wander, so "many a wake, and many a memorial?" Wander tells the story of the time he was at the bar a few years back and an Aussie came in. When asked how he'd heard of the place, the Aussie said that he'd befriended an old Irish gent named Paddy, who'd lived in New York City but had left in the 1920s and moved Down Under. Still, McSorley's had been so fondly remembered by old Paddy that when he died, he left money in his will for his Aussie friend to drink with at McSorley's, should he ever travel to the States. But not only expatriate New Yorkers love this pub. Pepe (the bartender) pulls out a letter from the Ukraine, congratulating McSorley's on its 150th anniversary. The writer had never been here but had heard of the place and had seen in the news of its anniversary.

It's easy to see why McSorley's charms and attracts. First of all, there's the history. It's not one out of books. It's plenty virtual. The longevity of the business, and the fact that it's always been family-run, help preserve that history. According to Bill Wander, Old John had the right idea to buy the building and to insist that nothing be changed in the way the business was run and in the way it looked inside. He was such a stickler for tradition that his son Bill would never consider any sort of renovation when he took over after his father died in 1910 at the age of 83. When carpenters told Bill McSorley the bar was falling apart and needed to be shored up, he sat in the kitchen, weeping for days, unable to eat or sleep until the workmen had finished.

But what started as a family's idiosyncrasy resulted in a pub that is truly authentic. There are the original ale pumps, the sawdust on the floor, the requisite house cat, and the chipped coffee mugs that substitute for a cash register. There are the portraits of Old John's heroes, the presidents and the prize fighters (Gentleman Jim Corbetts and John L. Sullivan's ale mugs still hang behind the bar.) There are the carved coconuts hanging from the ceiling, that Pepe laughingly calls "the Dalai Lama's head." Fellow bartender, poet, and author of *The McSorley Poems,* Geoffrey "Bart the Poet" Bartholomew writes that the coconuts are supposed to have been sent to Old John by Paul Gauguin, when the artist lived in Tahiti. There's the ancient safe that Old John kept his money in because he didn't trust banks. The potbellied stove that still warms the place, and the cheese, crackers, and onion plate that's been on the menu since the day the bar opened. (Old John ate a raw onion every day.) And the closing time, which is noteworthy in a city where bars can stay open until 4 a.m.: midnight on weekdays, and 1 a.m. on weekends. Closing time has been midnight almost every night since 1854 because Old John lived upstairs and wanted to go to bed early. He raised ten children upstairs, so it could be speculated that the city's population of McSorley's might have been lower had the closing time been later.

During Prohibition, Bill McSorley was never raided, he never paid a dime of protection money, and he continued to serve ale and porter, brewed by Barney Kelly in the basement. McSorley's ostensibly served only Fidelio's "near beer," which was legal. Perhaps that's why McSorley's was never raided, says Wander. Certainly, though, many an Irish cop during Prohibition had a drink at McSorley's, as their fathers may have before them. As for federal officials, who took over Prohibition enforcement after the first three years, they probably wouldn't be very interested in a little pub that wasn't serviced by bootleggers, whose identity and location were always prizes in any raid. So McSorley's passed through Prohibition without passwords, secret exits, or hideaways. The fact that McSorley's never closed its doors since 1854 is why some historians claim it is the oldest continually running bar in New York City.

In the late 1930s, Bill McSorley sold the bar to a cop by the name of Daniel O'Connell. O'Connell died 34 months later, one week after his daughter Dorothy's wedding to Harry Kirwan. Dorothy inherited the place. Before her father had died, however, she promised him that she would never set foot in McSorley's when it was open. It was a promise she always kept, says Wander. "Dorothy would come at night to pick Harry up and sit outside in the station wagon. And a couple of customers would always come out and ask her if she was going to come in, and she'd say 'maybe later,' but she never did." It was a tradition she honored even after the law made her father's dictum illegal. By that time, 1970, her son Danny was running the place. According to Wander, as soon as the law changed on August 10th of that year, he called her up and said "Mom, I want you to be the first woman served" and she refused, saying "I made a promise to my father." Now that's loyalty.

Danny Kirwan owned the bar until 1977, when current owner Matt Maher stepped in. He has preserved the interior, and the menu, and just about everything that makes McSorley's McSorley's. Like Old John, he is a lover of horses and has kept a few in his day. Like Old John, he protects the traditions and reveres the past, while keeping an eagle eye on those coin-holding coffee mugs. If Old John walked in, he'd recognize the place in an instant. Except for the women's room, put in in 1986, it's virtually the same. There's nothing about it that needed changing, says Maher. The idea is to run the bar, not ruin it. It's survived all these years because it is what it is. He says, "A pub is a pub." Well, a pub is a pub 'til it passes into legend, and that is what McSorley's has done. And as long as there are poets and writers, politicians and prize fighters, who need a place to lose time in, a legend it will remain.

REDUCERS
HEAP
YUENGLING

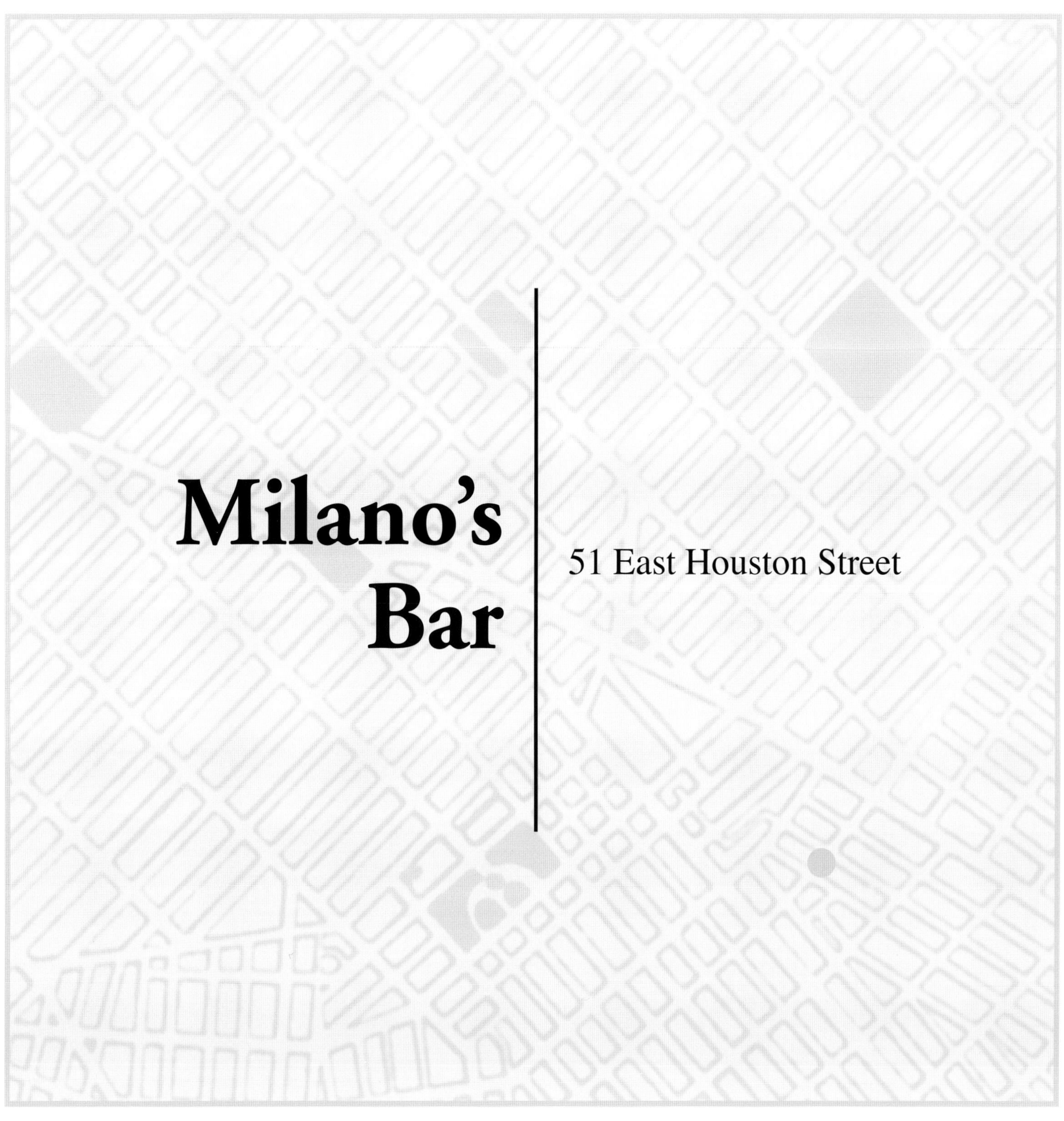

# Milano's Bar

51 East Houston Street

MILANO'S
BAR
GUINNESS
DRAUGHT
SIERRA NEVADA
ON TAP
Bass
Budweiser
Heineken
MILANO'S
HAPPY HOUR
WEEKDAYS
4PM-7PM
PULL
No Smoking
TIME'S UP

*Milano's is the last surviving Bowery bar, a leftover from the days when this neighborhood was packed with bars, flophouses, and the people who needed them.*

When owner Denis Lynch bought the place in 1988, it was the only bar left on Houston Street, and there were just three left on the Bowery. "In the 1940s and 1950s, there were 40 bars from Houston to Canal, " Lynch remembers. Bars were a good business back then, cheap to run. The rent on Milano's in 1972 was $75 a month, and on the Bowery, there were plenty of customers. Whether getting off the third shift and having an after work drink, or needing a stiff drink to face the day, Bowery residents headed to Milano's, here since 1923, and open at 7 a.m.

The decrease in the population of dive bars and flophouses might not seem so lamentable. But these places provided shelter and comfort for the poor, both idle and working. They made a community among those who lived on the fringes of society. Numbering around 35,000 at its peak, the residents of the mile-long Bowery were down-and-outs, mostly. This legendary skid row saw plenty of crime and criminals, though Lynch says his customers have always been a quiet, basically law-abiding bunch. Sure, there's the numbers running; there always has been since the days when the Old Police Headquarters was across the street, and the cops ran the rackets. Every once in a while one of the numbers runners hits it big and comes in and buys drinks for everyone. But Lynch maintains he's never had a robbery, never called the police on account of a disturbance here. Looking around at the regulars and bartender, friendly and unassuming, it's not hard to believe.

In this neighborhood, bars functioned as banks, too, for those whose credit was less than sterling. Bartenders and owners loaned money and cashed checks, along with running bar tabs, of course. "It's not so necessary these days," Lynch comments. Today's customer has less of a cash flow problem. Not like when the original owners, the Milano family, who ran the place for 65 years. Once, a regular who owed Tommy Milano some money was on his way into the bar to cash his welfare check. "He died on the sidewalk with the check in his hand," says Lynch. He adds, chuckling, "Let's hope he signed it over, first."

In the time since Lynch bought the place, the neighborhood went from hobo to boho. While there is still a core of regulars here at 9 a.m. having a quiet drink and reading the racing form, there are more SoHo and East Village types here in the evenings. They might be out for a good time and can appreciate the dive bar mystique that surrounds Milano's and the Bowery, but they have the money to pay for their pints of Guinness.

*While there is still a core of regulars here at 9 a.m. having a quiet drink and reading the racing form, there are more SoHo and East Village types here in the evenings.*

Guinness, by the way, was the first thing to be installed in Milano's when Denis Lynch took over, along with Bass and Harp. "When I got here, Tommy had six lines, all Schlitz," smiles Lynch. It was fifty cents a mug, but still, it was Schlitz—six taps of Schlitz—at that. Not the preferred lineup for any bar run by any son of the Auld Sod. Today Milano's offers Irish beer (as well as Brooklyn and Budweiser) for $5 a pint. With that, says Lynch, you get a clean glass. No charge for that, or for the atmosphere.

The atmosphere, such as it is, is provided not only by the clientele, but by the many photos lining the wall. The pictures are there both to decorate and to cover structural cracks that the Board of Health disapproves of. Photographers like the atmosphere, too—when they can fit inside, that is. Milano's interior is especially well-suited to black and white photography, and though a tight squeeze, has been used in photo shoots, most notably of Liam Neeson for *GQ* magazine.

Nobody was here taking pictures on September 11, 2001, though it turned out to be one of the City's most historic and most tragic days. Lynch was here at the opening, and there were about fifteen people at the bar at 9 a.m. By 10 a.m., the place was packed. People came in, some covered in dust, in shock. "We had people here drinking that day that never drank before in their lives," Lynch says, somberly. His daughter, who worked on the 68th floor of the World Trade Center, had taken the day off to celebrate her boyfriend's birthday, a fact that has forever endeared the young man to the Lynch family. On that day, the dust cloud from the collapse of the Twin Towers made its way up to Houston Street, and in it, a flood of humanity. They poured up the avenues, away from the disaster, stopping in at bars along the way. Milano's was busy all day long. Suddenly a whole lot of people were Bowery regulars, needing a stiff drink to face the day.

MULBERRY STREET
SARAH SKAGGS
DANCE
FRIDAY DECEMBER 15
DJ STEVEN HARVEY
ALL ARE INVITED!
Fresh Pond Road
Station
GUINNESS
WNB
Stereo 66
HARP
NEW AMSTERDAM

Heineken

# Molly's Pub and Restaurant, Shebeen

287 3rd Avenue

pub
·MOLLY'S·
RESTAURANT
SHEBEEN
MOLLY'S
SHEBEEN
Molly's
Lunch: 11am-4pm
Brunch: 12noon-4pm
(Sat & Sun)
Dinner: 4pm-til late

## *When you enter Molly's, you could swear you are in an authentic Irish pub—which you are. Well, sort of.*

It's owned and staffed by Irish folks and serves Irish food and drink. There's Irish football on the telly and frequently an Irish celebrity or politician stopping in for a drink. But this is New York City, and the interior, which looks centuries old, was actually constructed in 1964 by Stanley Franks, a well-known New York bar designer. It was created to look like an old Irish pub, and it does the job thoroughly, even down to the sawdust on the floor. You, along with the legions of other Molly's fans, will forgive the place its youth, it is an Irish pub with a real Irish pub feel—cool, dark, and mellow. And most importantly, that Irish feel of welcome. Just the place to duck into on a day when the weather or work is most unpleasant.

A cedar burning fireplace warms the pub in winter, and the staff does its bit to add to this warmth. One of the great things about Molly's is its staff, many of whom were here before current owners O'Connell and Ronaghan took over in 1991. It's this longevity that creates the familiarity among the patrons and staff, adding to the relaxed and fun atmosphere. It's a conversation bar. "You can hear your ears here," says O'Connell, smiling. The overall friendliness and quiet is probably a big reason for the bar's longevity and popularity. And don't forget the friendly pricing structure and generous drinks, leading to Molly's being voted "Best Pint of Guinness in New York" by *New York* magazine. That can't hurt.

*The overall friendliness and quiet is probably a big reason for the bar's own longevity and popularity.*

So, on any given afternoon, you may share a shepherd's pie and a pint with a neighborhood regular, a member of the Irish government, Mick O'Connell (legendary Irish footballer), and a record company executive. Or a future recording star: singer Diana Krall, (married to Elvis Costello, aka Declan McManus), was a regular here for years and wrote several songs sitting at a booth in Molly's. She came and gave out autographed CDs of her first album to the staff. Did Declan McManus himself ever bend an elbow here? O'Connell just smiles broader. The Clancy Brothers and Brendan Behan made Molly's their home over the years, as well. American stars have been spotted here, too, but honestly, they don't thrill the staff or owners the way the Irish celebs do. Then there's the Japanese. Japanese? "We were featured in Japanese *Playboy*," says O'Connell. So they've become a stop on several Japanese tours of bars in New York.

*"We were featured in Japanese* **Playboy,"** *says O'Connell.*

An authentic Irish pub that's popular with Irish ex-pats, New Yorkers, and Japanese tourists? As columnist Cindy Adams says, "Only in New York, folks, only in New York."

EXIT

# The Oak Room

59 West 44th Street
at the Algonquin Hotel

HOTEL
THE Algonquin

## *Once upon a time, Dorothy Parker, Robert Benchley, Heywood Broun, Alexander Woollcott, George S. Kaufman, Edna Ferber, Robert E. Sherwood, Marc Connolly, and Franklin P. Adams sat down to lunch at the Algonquin Hotel.*

And the rest, dear, is history. Literary history, that is—made during that meeting of wits and minds called the Round Table. Daily or almost, throughout the 1920s, these writers (several employed by *Vanity Fair*) would meet for this original and best-of-all-power-lunches, to talk, gossip, and trade barbs. Oh, and to help their friend, the editor Harold Ross, develop his pet project, a new magazine called *The New Yorker*. This they were happy to assist with. Ross's partner at the weekly Algonquin poker games had to lose quite a bit in order to secure the capital for Ross's venture.

The Round Table started just after World War I. Parker, Benchley, and Sherwood ate at the Pergola Room (now the Oak Room) at the Algonquin during their lunch breaks from *Vanity Fair*. When Alexander Woollcott returned to New York from his service as a war correspondent in 1919, the trio decided to have a roast of sorts for him. They invited several literary friends to heap insults upon Woollcott (who himself was known as a sharp-tongued critic) and, according to the Oak Room's Barbara McGurn, had the place decked out with bunting that spelled his name incorrectly, just to annoy him. Trouble was, McGurn tells it, he came from a very dysfunctional family and was used to being insulted, and so he ended up highly entertained by the whole affair. The event was carried off in such good spirits that the group (which would come to call itself the Vicious Circle) decided to meet regularly. They did, and it's a very good thing they did. American literature would never have been the same if they hadn't. Quite a claim for a little hotel bar, but it's true.

There is no other bar in town that can say that one of its regular lunch tables generated the kinds of fodder for newspaper and magazine columns that the Algonquin bar did. Quips and pranks from the Round Table were widely reported and quickly became legend. When Edna Ferber wore a suit similar to Noel Coward's (a frequent Round Table visitor), he commented on it immediately.

"You look almost like a man," he told her. "So do you," was Ferber's reply. When Benchley traveled to Venice, his telegram sent home to a friend was broadcast worldwide. It read: "Streets flooded. Please advise."

There has been a great deal written about the Round Table and its individual players. But perhaps *The Man Who Came to Dinner* sums up this world best. The play captures the kind of big egos and razor-sharp wits that the Round Table supported. A more recent film, stars Jennifer Jason Leigh called *Mrs. Parker and the Vicious Circle*, and gives good insight to the whole scene, too. How many bars have been so immortalized?

Because the Pergola became so crowded with visitors who wanted to observe the soon-to-be-immortal quips of the Round Table, Frank Case eventually moved the group to the nearby Rose Room (now the Round Table Room in honor of the group), where he seated them at a very large round table whose replica still exists.

The Algonquin became synonymous with sophistication and the quirkiness usually associated with writers or artists. Originally built in 1902 and run by a company "almost lost in history," notes McGurn, the hotel was located across from the Hippodrome, billed as the "world's largest playhouse." Soon to join the neighborhood were the Belasco, Broadhurst, Winthrop Ames, and 44th Street Theaters. Forty-fourth Street was home to the Harvard, Yale, New York Yacht, and Century Clubs, too, and Sherry's and Delmonico's were across the street at Fifth Avenue. But the greatest asset for the Algonquin came from the inside, the day before it opened, when Frank Case came to work there. Case convinced his boss to change the hotel's name from Puritan to Algonquin. (The name "Puritan" sounded too stiff to Case.) He was to turn the hotel into a legendary hostelry, as he worked his way up from desk clerk to owner (bought for $1,250,000) by 1926. He owned the Algonquin until 1946, when he died.

Case loved actors and writers, finding in them personalities sympathetic to his own. He also found they offered cachet to his establishment. Booth Tarkington, Douglas Fairbanks, Sr., John Barrymore, and H. L. Mencken all stayed or lived here. (Mary Pickford and Fairbanks, Sr., were particular friends of Case's, and Douglas Fairbanks, Jr. grew up here.) Under his stewardship the "Gonk" became the beloved idiosyncratic spot it is. In the lobby is a grandfather clock that he once accepted in lieu of payment back in 1910, and there is always an Algonquin cat living in the hotel, visiting guests at its whim. The first Algonquin cat was adopted by Case back in the thirties. The current hotel cat, Matilda, receives her own fan mail.

According to McGurn, the Algonquin was way ahead of its time, as hotels go. Women were welcome even when traveling alone, which was unusual. Gertrude Stein and Alice B. Toklas, Simone de Beauvoir, Eudora Welty, Maya Angelou, and Helen Hayes rested heads on Algonquin pillows, and actress Tallulah Bankhead's senator grandfather wouldn't let his daughter stay anywhere else when she came to New York to seek her fame. Famous opera singer Marian Anderson was a guest here, at a time when African-Americans were prohibited from many hotels in the city. Like all famous watering holes, the Gonk attracted the greatest literary minds of the day, including Nobel laureates Sinclair Lewis (who wanted to buy the hotel), Derek Walcott, and William Faulkner (who wrote his Nobel acceptance speech in the Algonquin lobby in 1950) and athletes flocked here as well, including Gene Tunney and Frank Shields (the tennis star and Brooke's grandfather).

Even before Prohibition, which by McGurn's reckoning "perfectly coincided with the Round Table," no liquor was served to members of the Round Table during their daily lunch. Presumably, however, Algonquin guests could always secure liquor for in-room consumption, but Case decided it was best to keep his writers sober during the day. Unfortunately for chef James Beard, Prohibition was repealed by the time he came to work at *Gourmet* magazine. His editor didn't like the amount of time Beard frittered away at the Algonquin bar, and so he was fired, starting a feud that lasted twenty years.

After lunch at the Algonquin, the gang would head over to artist Neysa McMein's apartment. She kept a still there and that's when the day's drinking would begin. The day usually ended at '21,' the club of choice for Benchley and Parker, among many others. As the 1930s approached, and the Round Table crowd began to thin, Hollywood called. Still, while it lasted, no bar boasted a more illustrious table.

In 1939, Frank Case opened the Oak Room in the Algonquin as a supper club. It drew a pretty fabulous and diverse crowd, with a guest list that started at Greta Garbo. In 1941, Case closed the Oak Room and it remained closed until 1980. In 1946, Case died. His books, *Tales from a Wayward Inn* and *Do Not Disturb*, which chronicled his life at the Algonquin, were both best sellers.

The next owner, Ben Bodne, was a South Carolina millionaire. Bodne had honeymooned at the Algonquin in 1924 and promised his wife Mary that one day they would own the place. He fulfilled that honeymoon promise in 1946 when he bought the hotel from Case's estate. (The honeymoon promise he'd made to himself—that he'd one day own a major league baseball team—fell by the wayside, however.) Bodne's devotion to the Algonquin never wavered over the forty-plus-years he owned it. (Mary, incidentally, was from Charleston and knew George Gershwin from the days when he was writing the music for *Porgy and Bess*.) The Bodnes lovingly ran the Gonk until 1990. While they made many updates and improvements to the hotel, perhaps the greatest thing they did was reopen the Oak Room in 1980, giving New York one of its greatest cabaret spaces.

Another great thing they did was hire Barbara McGurn to book acts. Like Case, she is an eccentric, larger-than-life personality who fits in perfectly at the Algonquin. It is she who has been globe-and-country-trotting, finding the kinds of cabaret acts that have made the Oak Room what *New York* magazine calls "New York's Best Cabaret," and what the *Times of London* lovingly refers to as "the holy of holies for cabaret performers." An ardent Boston Red Sox fan, McGurn can talk baseball and jazz with the best of them, and looks after her talent like a mother hen does her chicks. She has found and nurtured more cabaret stars than probably anyone in New York, or in the world, for that matter.

> *It is she who has been globe-and-country-trotting, finding the kinds of cabaret acts that have made the Oak Room what New York magazine calls "New York's Best Cabaret"...*

McGurn remembers when her good friend, the *New York Times* music critic Stephen Holden, called her up in 1989 and told her to get down to the Village to a club called the Knickerbocker. "There's a boy down there who's a beauty and a terrific pianist," he told her. The boy with the chops was Harry Connick, Jr. McGurn persuaded

Connick to come to the Oak Room, where he was catapulted into the cabaret firmament. Michael Feinstein also debuted here, in 1986. McGurn laughs to recall the mixed crowds at Michael's shows which included Brooke Astor, Jacqueline Onassis, David Susskind, Leonard Bernstein, Fiat's Gianni Agnelli (who hired Feinstein to play at his annual party at the Palace in St. Moritz), Liberace, and Roy Cohn, wheeled in his chair by his nurse.

The Oak Room roster includes Karen Akers, Sylvia McNair, and of course, the incomparable "Callas of Cabaret," Andrea Marcovicci. But mixed in with the legendary song stylists are always McGurn's rookies, those rising stars she is so good at catching. In addition to Feinstein, Connick, and Marcovicci, stars launched here include John Pizzarelli, Diana Krall, Tierney Sutton, Peter Cincotti and young British phenom Jamie Cullum.

Writers and artists haven't been forgotten at the Algonquin. There are suites named after James Thurber and Dorothy Parker, which contain facsimiles of letters, original prints, as well as other artifacts and memorabilia. (The Parker letters, found recently, have never been published.) The Spoken Word series, featuring best-selling authors, goes on yearly, as well as the Thurber Award ceremonies for the best book of American humor. The Estate of Noel Coward helped the Algonquin decorate and commemorate the Noel Coward Suite, dedicated in December 2005 with the British Consule General officiating, followed by an all-star Coward Cabaret in the Oak Room. Hoping to encourage new writers, installed in the lobby is a writer's table, with data port available. All those famous writers with their famous thoughts, absorbed into the paneling. The ghosts of those Round Tablers sort of brush up against you, like Matilda the cat.

To celebrate the arrival of the writer's table, Nat Benchley, Robert's grandson, and Tony Adams, Frank P. Adams's son, were on hand. McGurn saw to it that the Algonquin's years were appropriately chronicled in song. "We began with a song from 1902, from the era of Diamond Jim Brady and Lillian Russell," says McGurn. And ended with—what else? She smiles. "Thanks for the Memories," of course.

UZZARDS BAY
JULY 19
EEK STARTING
JULY 19, 20, 21
AN FONTAINE
TYRONE
ALL
JULY 22
Maker's Mark
ROUX
NEW YORK
PUB QUIZ

# Old Town Bar & Restaurant

45 East 18th Street

OLD TOWN
BAR
RESTAURANT
NO PARKING
ACTIVE DRIVEWAY

*A setting that calls to mind a Scott Joplin tune, the Old Town Bar & Restaurant is absolutely vintage, Gilded Age New York.*

It's been around since 1892, when Union Square had a railroad station, and German restaurants were common in this neighborhood. Originally called Viemeister's, the restaurant was a bit less fancy than the famous Luchow's Restaurant, which was located on 14th Street. Viemeister's featured German cuisine, served both at the (men-only) bar downstairs and the family dining room upstairs. During Prohibition it was a speakeasy, hiding in plain sight as Craig's Restaurant. The booths in the barroom still have seats that lift up, a holdover from those days when customers needed a place to hide booze in a hurry. Then in 1933, Claus Lohden bought the place and changed the name to Old Town. His son Henry and daughter-in-law Bernice eventually took over. When Henry died, Bernice stayed on as part owner, along with partner and former manager/bartender Lawrence Meagher and his son Gerard.

Their devotion to keeping the interior and exterior just as it was has paid off in Old Town's enduring popularity, both as a watering hole and as a set for films and commercials. In fact, if you spend any time watching TV, will see snippets of the Old Town Restaurant. Most frequently seen in the old intro on *Late Night with David Letterman* when it aired on NBC, the Old Town was also known as Riff's Bar in *Mad About You*. The perfectly preserved interior has brought Hollywood in several times, to film such movies as *The Devil's Own*, *Bullets Over Broadway*, and *The Last Days of Disco*. The atmosphere is genuine nineteenth Century New York, with frosted glass doors, tile floors and a gorgeous mahogany bar. According to Gerard Meagher, the bar was built by Rieger and Son, a firm that

> *In fact, if you spend any time watching TV, you can see snippets of the Old Town Restaurant.*

built many bars in the city. An identical one to Old Town's was located on 19th Street and was long ago sold off. Fortunately for patrons and movie lovers alike, the well-preserved Old Town bar still stands where it always has. So much has the interior been left on its own that the ceiling, last painted white on Election Day 1952, is stained a dark brown, thanks to years of cigar and cigarette smoke. Sort of makes you feel better about having one of Old Town's famous burgers.

*Fortunately for patrons and movie lovers alike, the well-preserved Old Town Restaurant and Bar still stands.*

The old time atmosphere at the Old Town Restaurant has attracted its share of writers along the way, and there are plenty of framed signed book covers to testify to that, including those from Frank McCourt, Seamus Heaney, Thomas Kelly, and Jim Dwyer. Food is delivered to the bar via dumbwaiters, and the longtime bar staff keeps even the thirstiest writer amply supplied. The only thing that's missing is a piano playing a Scott Joplin tune.

45

# Onieal's Grand Street Bar

174 Grand Street

*Set in a neighborhood that for more than a hundred years was the knife's edge of wealth, corruption, poverty, and crime, Onieal's today is a refined, hip restaurant with a history.*

The bar is directly opposite the old police headquarters. Its former occupations as a brothel, speakeasy, and gambling parlor would seem to have been opposed to the purpose of the police department—but see, that's the corruption part. So endemic was this corruption (we're talking the heyday of Tammany Hall) that when the police headquarters was built in 1909, a tunnel was dug connecting the buildings to allow cops to step across the street for some cheer. The tunnel, which ended up coming in very handy during Prohibition, is still visible in Onieal's and is used as a wine cellar. The tunnel has been filled in by the new owners of the old headquarters building, which now houses very ritzy condos, filled with tenants such as Steffi Graf, Winona Ryder, and Christy Turlington.

There's been a bar on this site since 1875, and over the years it was also called Callahan's and the Dutchman. It was best known as The Press Room, however, after the Headquarters was built and reporters needed a joint to hang out in to keep an eye on who was coming and going across the street—Al Capone and John Dillinger among the most notorious. Teddy Roosevelt, police commissioner from 1895 to 1897, was a frequent visitor to the bar. Whether he availed himself of the services of the ladies upstairs is unknown, but every effort was made to lure men up there. According to Onieal's owner, Chris Onieal, during renovations it was discovered that originally there had been no plumbing for toilets on the ground floor, only upstairs. He speculates that this was done deliberately, to entice bar patrons to the upper floors. A staircase to the upstairs rooms ran from the basement tunnel through the bar.

A bordello, yes, and a fine one. The rooms upstairs were small but with large windows overlooking the street (for advertising purposes). Downstairs, the elaborately-carved mahogany ceiling, imported from Venice, features four grinning devils' heads. Originally the bar was circular and in the center of the room, and there were no windows, just the door for a glimpse of the outside. When the police headquarters relocated in 1973, the bar lost its best customers, and the reporters also stopped hanging out there.

*When the police headquarters relocated in 1973, the bar lost its best customers, and the reporters also stopped hanging out there.*

So The Press Room went out of business, and the bar lay empty for a while before it became an Italian restaurant. When the folks who ran the restaurant opened the place, says Onieal, they found ledgers from the days when it was a gambling den. They passed the ledgers on to the New York Historical Society. Chris bought the place in 1994 and renovated and polished 'til the bar was ready. Onieal's Grand Street Bar's location (two blocks from Chinatown, one from Little Italy, and one from SoHo) and its history have ensured its continuing popularity. The interior is sleek, but warm, and so appealing that it was used as a set for a TV show, in which it was known as a bar named "Scout," owned by characters known as Steven and Aidan. As befits a place with this kind of history, the show's name was *Sex and the City.*

MEN
TAP
McSorley's
Bottle
AMSTEL
Corona
Becks
BASS & CO PALE ALE

# P & G Cafe

279 Amsterdam Avenue

CAFE
STEAKS
CHOPS
BAR
Yuengling
NO SMOKING

*An old beauty, still with a lot to offer, P & G Cafe has been a classic New York neighborhood bar in a classic New York neighborhood, the Upper West Side, for more than 60 years.*

Though genial owner Tom Chahalis smiles and says "It could use a little fixing up," the truth is when you love someone, you don't really notice the wrinkles, and that is how the regulars feel about the P & G. Think of it as you would an old actor: worn around the edges, but interesting, the wear and tear adding layers of character.

P & G Cafe was opened in 1942 by Tom's grandfather, also named Tom Chahalis, and his two sons, Pete and George Chahalis (hence the P and the G.) They bought the place when it was called Phalen's, a bar that had been there since 1933. The name of the bar before that isn't recorded, but Tom says it was known to be a gambling parlor and speakeasy during Prohibition. There was a series of rooms, complete with a men's and a women's restroom, down in what is now the basement. "We found graffiti on the walls downstairs when we bought the place, Dutch Schultz's and Bugsy Siegel's." he says. The graffiti is covered up now, just like the mural that once covered the entire interior. Painted in 1942 by an Austrian artist, the painting was a pastoral landscape, complete with waterfalls, forest, animals, and blue sky with clouds and geese. "He painted the whole thing from memory," remembers Tom. "It was like you walked into the forest when you came in." Today all that remains visible of the mural is the back wall; the rest is under the drop ceiling tiles or paneling. Hidden beauty, layers of character.

Tom started working at P & G in 1957, but then headed out to Los Angeles to try his luck. Lucky he was, landing a job at a well-known bar frequented by Hollywood elite. His roommate in the early sixties was Max Baer, Jr., famous for playing the role of Jethro in the TV series *The Beverly Hillbillies*, the number one rated show in 1969. Tom even had a hand in Baer getting the role. Chahalis had run into a friend of his who worked for one of the talent agencies, and the guy told him they were casting for a new series and were looking for a tall, athletic actor who could play

guitar. Tom went home and told Baer, who at first felt he wasn't well suited to the role, as he didn't play guitar. But Chahalis insisted he audition. "I told him, 'they're looking for someone tall,' and he was 6 foot 4, so he should try." Baer went for the audition, and the rest is in every TV trivia book known to man. "You should have seen the phone calls between Donna Douglas (Ellie May) and Max every day, while they waited to hear if they got the job," notes Chahalis. Having an actor for a roommate and actors for customers meant a constant stream of the up-and-coming and the rich and famous. Chahalis played on the Show League softball team. The team roster read like the Fall TV Preview for TV Guide, including names like James Garner and Mike Connors. It was a lot of fun, but his dad back at the P & G needed him, so to New York he returned.

Time in Hollywood gave Chahalis a taste for theater folk. He ended up owning a bar two doors down from the stage door of the Palace Theater on 47th Street. Called Gus & Andy's, it was frequented by actors, becoming a second home to anyone playing at the Palace. This was in the early to mid sixties, so the crowd included some of the legends of Broadway. The original cast of *Sweet Charity* practically lived at Gus & Andy's. Star Gwen

Verdon and director Bob Fosse (who at the time were married) became close friends. "Gwen used to call me up and ask me to bring her some chicken and orange juice," remembers Chahalis. "As a joke, I'd put on one of the bartender's uniforms and serve her in it. She'd be lying on her chaise, in her dressing room, good-humoredly playing the queen, which she pretty much was, of Broadway, anyway." Remembers fellow cast member Marie Wallace, "Gwen had a birthday coming up, and we wanted to do something special at her party…Most of us hung out at a restaurant called Gus & Andy's, which was right next door to the Palace backstage entrance on 47th Street, and that's where we had the party." A memorable night unfolded, part of a very memorable time. There's a party going on every night on Broadway, and if you own a bar there, your role is host. When you've got celebrities Marvin Hamlisch, Bob Fosse, and Gwen Verdon hanging out at your place, it just doesn't get better than that.

The famous Black Out of 1965 was a great night at the P & G and Gus & Andy's. "It was a party, just a huge party, all over the city," smiles Chahalis. "We gave out plates of food, what could you do with it? There was no refrigeration…People partied in the streets, and they were so nice to each other." Of course, as the liquor flowed and the night grew dark, mishaps did happen. "We ran next door to the church and asked the Reverend for some candles, but they were out. So we tried to fashion oil lamps using steel pitchers and some corn oil from the kitchen. We put rags in and lit the rags and whoosh, the flames went so high that they charred the ceiling! I had to have painters come in the next day and paint it." Like many New Yorkers, though, "The Night the Lights Went Out" is forever etched in Chahalis's mind as one of the great nights in New York.

After Chahalis sold Gus & Andy's, and when they were redoing Rockefeller Center, the circle of theater friends followed him uptown, where they have been ever since. The P & G is located in one of the most musical neighborhoods in the world, just across from Verdi Square, with Mannes College of Music around the corner and The Julliard School and Lincoln Center right up the street. The bar is one of those unassuming places where actors can relax. Laughs Chahalis, "Cindy Hughes was a Rockette and a good friend, and she used to come here with all the girls, and they'd do a kick line right here in the dining room while everyone at the bar sang 'New York, New York.'"

> *"…they'd do a kick line right here in the dining room while everyone at the bar sang 'New York, New York.'"*

The P & G was a favorite with actors and theater people, as well as its regulars. Reasonable prices, good food, and an actor-friendly atmosphere were enough to guarantee a steady flow. Not just Broadway types, but Hollywood too—as disparate as rock legend Meatloaf ("He used to eat three of our 8 ounce burgers at one sitting!" says Chahalis), Cher, Leonard Nimoy, and Christopher Walken. Like a character actor, the P & G is a bit typecast and has often played the role of New York bar in shows like *Seinfeld* and *Will and Grace*, as well as the films *Donnie Brasco* anda *Runaway Bride*. Like a character actor, it does the job without fanfare, blending into the background, yet adding an interesting note to every performance of that play called New York City.

PARIS CAFE EST. 1873
116

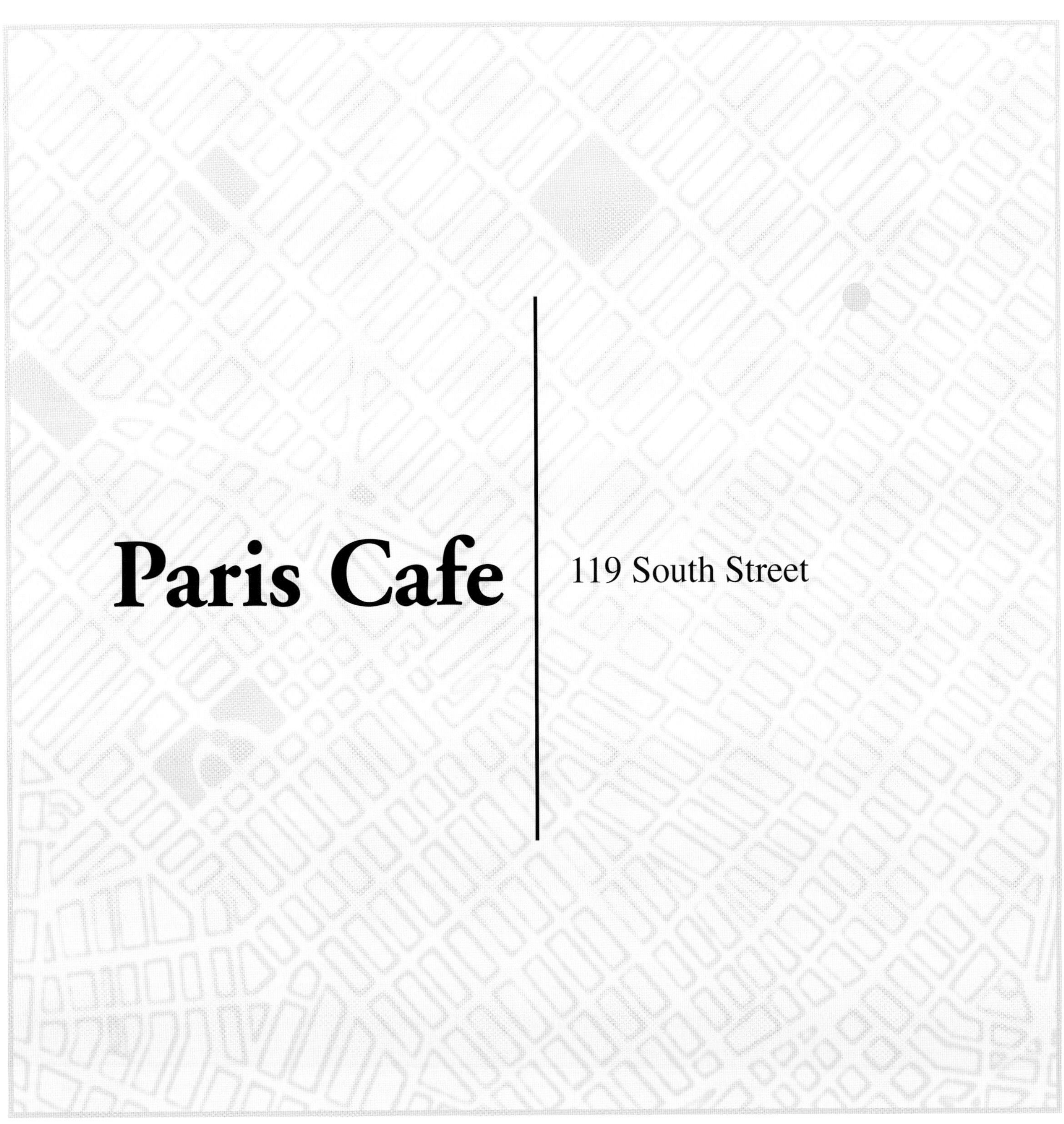

# Paris Cafe

119 South Street

Cyberfile
HEINEKEN
GUINNESS

*When John Roebling's marvel of engineering, the Brooklyn Bridge, opened to traffic in 1883, celebrations were held all along the waterfront in Manhattan and Brooklyn.*

One notable party was held atop the swanky Meyer's Hotel on South Street and featured celebrity guests Annie Oakley and Buffalo Bill Cody. After the party and fireworks subsided, the guests repaired downstairs to the hotel's bar, an elegant little spot in the middle of the rough and tumble seaport. Meyers, a restaurateur, had opened the hotel ten years earlier with a view to providing fine accommodations in a corner of the city where they were sorely lacking. Meyers catered to the upscale crowd and spared no expense in fitting up the rooms or the bar downstairs. Beautiful fabrics, wood, mirrors, and tiles were used to furnish the cafe, and the bar was hand carved and imported from Austria. To suit the stylish ambience he strove to create, Meyers named his bar Paris Café.

The list of patrons reads like the cast of characters from *Ragtime*. Diamond Jim Brady and Thomas Edison used Paris Cafe as a home away from home, and some of Edison's earliest films are taken of the docks and East River. Says owner John Ronaghan, "He used it as a second office," when designing the world's first centralized power station on nearby Pearl Street. Teddy Roosevelt was a regular while he was police commissioner. Criminals and anarchists played and plotted here as well—Butch Cassidy and the Sundance Kid stayed here, journalist John Reed held secret meetings upstairs during the 1920s, and during the 1930s, Murder, Inc. kingpins Albert Anastasia and Louis "Lepke" Buchalter used the Paris as a base. The docks being nearby and under mob control made the location logical.

*Criminals and anarchists played and plotted here as well–Butch Cassidy and the Sundance Kid stayed here, journalist John Reed held secret meetings upstairs during the 1920s…*

According to retired mail carrier Richard McGorty, who worked the seaport route for 35 years, mob control extended to the business, too. Paris Cafe became a hangout for mobsters, and for years, numbers and other rackets ran out of it. "It had a bad reputation," says McGorty. "The place was full of loan sharks and gamblers…The bartender back then was a big bald guy named Curly." Even Curly wasn't tough enough to keep the Paris from being raided for numbers running, and during the early 70s, it was consequently shut down.

A few years later, a group of artists opened the place and named it The Sketchpad. Remembers McGorty, "They put brown paper on the tables and gave you crayons, and if you drew a picture good enough to go on the wall, you'd get a free meal." Cute idea, considering how artists are usually starving. After it sold, Pat MacMenamin and Jimmy O'Neill ran it, just as the South Street Seaport opened in the 80s.

*The new owners refurbished the inside, and even installed heated bar rails to warm their customers' feet on damp nights.*

MacMenamin and O'Neill decided to keep the place open 24 hours. Nights they catered to the trade a the Fulton Fish Market, and days to the tourists at the Seaport. The new owners refurbished the inside, and even installed heated bar rails to warm their customers' feet on damp nights. This arrangement was a better business formula than giving away free food for a pretty picture. Paris Cafe enjoyed an around-the-clock crowd, and it was once again the 'in' spot on the docks. Eventually MacMenamin sold it and opened his Irish pub around the corner. Four years ago O'Connell and Ronaghan took over.

Ronaghan and O'Connell have seen some changes down here, mostly in the decline of the Fulton Fish Market. Now down to 2,000 workers from a peak of 5,000, the area is increasingly going the way of expensive residential units. In late 2005, the Market, which had been on this site for more than 200 years, moved to Hunts Point, The Bronx. The fact that it is the longest-running market in North America isn't enough to stand in the way of progress. Sighs O'Connell, "It's a shame, really, because it's real New York, and there's nothing like it anywhere. You have to come down here at four in the morning to truly appreciate it." The sights, the sounds, and of course the smells, of this market. Tense and busy as an emergency room it, bursts open late at night, as the boats come in and unload. Third and fourth generations working the same stalls, the air filled with shouts and curses, the diesel fumes of the forklifts whizzing through the crowds, the narrow lanes bustling with fishermen and fishmongers, market bosses and chefs from the City's finest restaurants. The scene, says McGorty, is unparalleled. Like a lot of New Yorkers, the men at Paris Cafe describe the passing of the Fish Market as another step away from old New York. The warehouses are being converted into lofts and condos. McGorty points out that the shift from a commercial area to a residential one is best understood by the weight of his mail bag. "When I started carrying mail down here, there were about 3,000 residential deliveries. Now there are 20,000." Still, for Paris Cafe, more housing means more customers. The kind that work in the nearby Financial District and keep bankers'—not fishermen's—hours.

19
PUSH

BAR GRILL
317

Pabst Blue Ribbon
PARKSIDE LOUNGE MAY
NO SMOKING
It's Miller Time
POOL

# Parkside Lounge

317 East Houston Street

Give the gift of Booze!
TO:
FROM:
Cocktail!
JESS
ADRIANE
Bobby
Chris Jay
ROSIE
PARKSIDE
JULIE
JAMIE
KAREN
NEAL
thanks
Marissa
Racheal
NEALE
GRACEN
K&A
Birthday Beer
MAY
EVENTS
Ask For Imported
BLUE NUN
By The Glass
00.00
NCR

*Parkside Lounge is one of the best little hangouts in New York City.*

One of the most important jobs at the Parkside is keeping track of the many bands and comics that perform, as well as running a tab of drinks comp'd by the regulars for the regulars. The complimentary drinks are tallied on a board over the bar, so if you're lucky enough to be a regular at the Parkside, you may walk in and learn that one of your esteemed colleagues has already paid for a drink for you.

And there have been ghosts spotted here, such as blood dripping off the ceiling tiles, and hard-to-reach compressors down in the basement getting unplugged. "The Parkside electrical ghost" is what owner Karen Waltermire calls it. "The lights and sound would go off during a [band's] set sometimes, for no reason," she says (though maybe the ghost was a music critic). There were other poltergeists—things going missing and turning up in weird spots, names being called out from the empty upstairs. Was the spirit left from the time when the basement was an East River ice house, perhaps a worker who died down there? Or a lost soul from the days when the tunnels, now filled in, were in use, probably by the Underground Railroad?

Maybe the ghost hearkened from the Parkside's drag queen heyday. Back in the fifties, the Parkside Lounge's former owner, Marty Gellerman, was one of the first bar owners to hire blacks and gay men. Gays and drag queens frequented the bar, along with, in the bad days, the drugs-and-numbers running crowd. When Waltermire took over in 1996, she had one of the more famous local drag queens, Miss Sweetie, run a drag queen party each week. Lavitia, in her trademark Mary Poppins hat, was a fixture at these events, along with most of the Village drag celebs.

It was during this period that the Williamsburg Bridge was being renovated. A bunch of very macho construction workers ate lunch here frequently, until one day a couple of teenagers walked by and

saw all the men inside wearing sleeveless t-shirts and construction hats—kind of like, well, the Village People. Remembers bartender Audrey, "They looked in and said to each other, 'Hey, I didn't know this was a gay bar!'" She adds, chuckling, "The construction workers ate in a hurry and left."

Ghosts and drag queens aside, live music is what the Parkside Lounge is known for most, though the bar also hosts regular stand-up comedy and open mike nights. Tour and studio musicians between gigs, as well as stage performers, like to play here. There's a 1,000 square foot room in the back, with good acoustics, sound system, and stage—they do it *right* here. They don't just clear tables and stick the band in the corner. Waltermire has a genuine appreciation for music and musicians, and bands know it. The Parkside has become one of the hot smaller venues in the city.

Every night offers a chance to see so-and-so, who plays for you-know-who. James Wormworth (*Late Night with Conan O'Brien*), Clark Gayton (Sting), Shawn Pelton (*SNL*), and Brian Mitchell (Roseanne Cash). There's Bill Sims, Jr., Buddy Merriam, new E-Streeter Soozie Tyrell, and Tony Trischka, "one of the Bluegrass deities," Waltermire says proudly. Given the caliber of performers, it's only natural that the audience be equally stellar: Björk, David Byrne, Janeane Garofalo, William Hurt, Sir William McKellar, Moby, Sean Penn, and John Goodman have spent some time Parkside. Oh yeah, "and the *3rd Rock from the Sun* chick, you know, the tall one," Waltermire remembers. While it's always great to have special guest stars at your joint, she knows that it's the regulars who make this the Parkside. Some of them, like Bob Saldana, have been coming here for decades.

Waltermire worked at the Bitter End in the Village for years, and was their first female bartender. She cut her teeth booking acts there and decided to try it on her own. In 1996, she bought the Parkside. "I came here to run this place with live music," Waltermire says. No DJs, thank you very much. For artistic advice, she collaborated with Gordon Gaines, who died before he could fulfill his duties as the Parkside's first artist-in-residence. The Parkside Lounge holds fundraisers to support its memorial to Gaines, which donates instruments to P.S. 140 and sends kids to music camp each year. Today musician Brian Mitchell is the artist-in-residence, and like all the people associated with the lounge, is a friend as well as a colleague. Her bartenders and managers are usually artists, actors, or musicians, kindred spirits to Waltermire. "The only people that work for me are people I want to be with," she adds, and manager Peter Abraham agrees. Some of the bartenders, like actor Christopher, work here mostly for the fun of it. "I used to drink here, and then I decided it'd be fun to work here, too," he says. Turns out he was right. After all, this is a hangout. And to be a member at this clubhouse, all you have to do is show up, be friendly, and have fun. Kewl.

> *"The only people that work for me are people I want to be with."*

OLDEST ORIGINAL BAR
IN NEW YORK CITY
OPENED 1864
Smoking

# Pete's Tavern

129 East 18th Street

Pete's Tavern
EST. 1864
Since Abe Lincoln was president
3 DINING ROOMS IN REAR
FRIENDS OF LIBRARIES U.S.A.
PETE'S TAVERN
EST. 1864
Barkeep recalls John's curiosity
The Dish
PETE'S

*As longtime bartender Buster Smith likes to say, "Sooner or later, everyone comes to Pete's."*

Seeing as how Pete's is *one* of the oldest, if not *the* oldest, continually operating bars in New York, he's probably not exaggerating. And even if you've never been here, you'd recognize it immediately. When Hollywood or Madison Avenue needs a bar for a set, they come to Pete's. It's been featured in countless TV shows and films: *Ragtime*, *Endless Love*, *Law & Order*, *Sex and the City*, and is such a quintessential New York bar, it's been in several beer commercials. So whether it's in person or through the magic of media, Buster Smith is right—sooner or later, everybody comes to Pete's.

Pete's Tavern is located in a building that dates from 1829, but was probably serving liquor as early as 1852, when it was listed on city records as a "grocery store." If it was serving liquor in 1852, then it is the oldest continually-run drinking establishment in the city. Officially, though, the tavern first opened in 1864. It hasn't closed since.

Originally called the Portman Hotel, it was bought in 1899 by Tom and John Healy, who ran it until 1921. Healy's was a favorite hangout of O. Henry's, appearing in his short story "The Lost Blend" as "Kenealy's." "The Gift of the Magi" was written here, too, in Booth 3. "People call up and ask 'Can I reserve the O. Henry booth?'" chuckles Smith. A copy of the original story is framed over the booth, along with some old photos of days gone by at the bar. In addition to inspiring O. Henry, Ludwig Bemelmans wrote *Madeline* here. (Its famous opening line "In an old house in Paris that was covered with vines…" was written on the back of one of Pete's menus.) A plaque out front from the Friends of Libraries USA attests to the "nurturing environment" that Pete's has provided writers over the years.

During Prohibition, Pete's operated its saloon in the back room, with the front of the bar used as a flower shop. The bar was thinly disguised, to say the least. The bar entrance was conspicuously marked by a long awning and elegant carpet to the curb. Pretty fancy entrance for a flower shop. As manager John Reynolds says, "They didn't kill themselves changing the façade. I almost laugh when I look at the pictures."

Of course, politicians drank here throughout Prohibition, especially Mayor Jimmy Walker. More impressive though, is Pete's political hat trick: Joe Kennedy, Sr. provided the bootleg liquor during Prohibition, Jack and Jackie patronized Pete's, and John Kennedy, Jr. became a Pete's regular after seeing a photo on the wall of his parents sitting at a booth here.

Buster Smith came on as bartender in 1968, when he retired from the NYPD. "I'd been the cop on the Irving Place beat since '48," he recalls. "I knew Pete Belles (for whom Pete's was named) when he owned it." Belles later sold the joint to Johnny White and Jimmy Musso, who sold it to Helen and James Frawley. In 1980, Bruce Friedman's dad, Dave, bought it, and it's been in the family ever since. Smith has seen them come and seen them go, always coming in for his shifts regularly, always watching over the crowd. Even at his age, he looks like he can still keep a crowd in check. You get the feeling he knows what to do with the business end of a baseball bat if things "get busy." But they don't, he says. "It's quiet here, no trouble." He should know. It's a crowd he's known for almost sixty years, a mix of all types over the years: hippies, Teamsters, college kids, rich folks, neighborhood people, movie stars, politicians, and crazies. It's been quite a run for Buster Smith. He doesn't think of retiring, however. Each shift is different, interesting. Because you never know who might come in. After all, sooner or later, everyone comes to Pete's.

*Even at his age, he looks like he can still keep a crowd in check. You get the feeling he knows what to do with the business end of a baseball bat if things "get busy."*

O. HENRY
wrote...
GIFT OF THE MAGI
1905

WINES • CLARKE'S • LIQUORS
CLARKE'S
P.J. Clarke's
Est. 1884
Clarke's

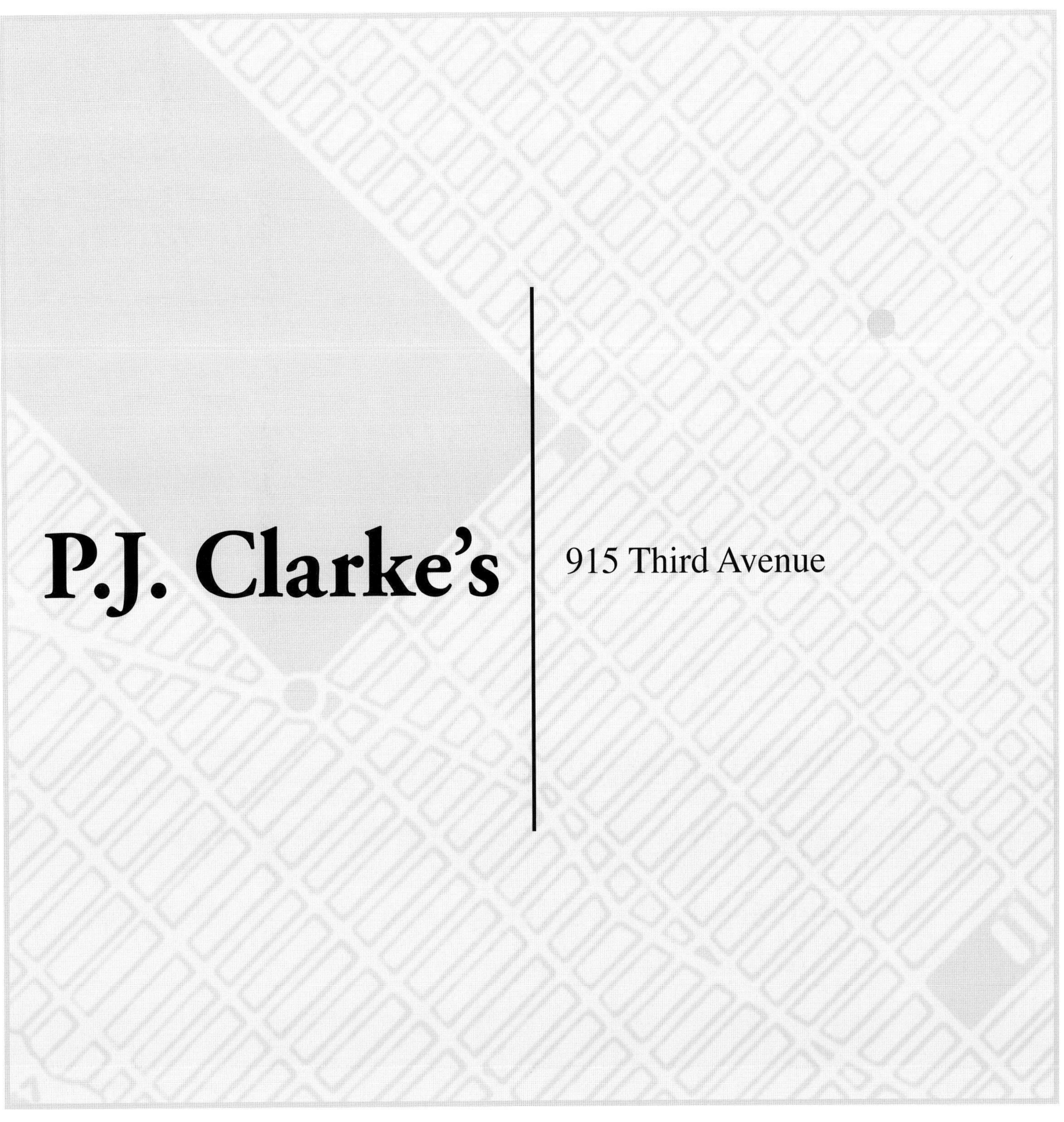

# P.J. Clarke's

915 Third Avenue

Auxiliary to Sons of
Union Veterans of the Civil War
LADIES

*Like something out of a children's book, P. J. Clarke's is the little bar that could. Founded in 1884, when this neighborhood was vastly different, Clarke's was an ordinary tavern that worked its way through some pretty extraordinary times.*

It plugged away, remaining essentially the same while its neighborhood struggled through two World Wars, The Depression, Prohibition, and perhaps toughest of all, the jungle that is New York real estate. It survived those battles and stands today, a Victorian curlicue of a building in the midst of sleek stone and glass towers. An Irish tweed jacket in a sea of Armani.

Some say adaptation breeds success, but in P. J. Clarke's case, unswerving consistency has been its formula. As the neighborhood changed from teeming slum to Midtown East, as the cavernous foundations for the great office complexes were dug, Clarke's kept on as a simple saloon. Food fashions came and went. P. J. Clarke's rode the undulating wave of popularity, up in the go-go sixties, down in the lean late nineties. Through it all, the bartenders were surly, the food was cheap and good, and the beer cold. No constant changes of theme or menu here. For one thing, the regulars wouldn't have stood for it. Neither would the tourists, the celebrities, and the office workers who have increasingly discovered P. J. Clarke's authentic spirit. Even if the owners had wanted to change the old place, the customers wouldn't have let them.

When it was bought in 2002 by a group of investors (including Timothy Hutton, Phillip Scotti, and George Steinbrenner), the regulars were wary. Especially when the new owners closed the place and put up scaffolding for a year. But the new owners were as concerned with meeting the regulars' approval as they were the city inspectors'—or almost. The renovation was such a success, folks didn't believe it had happened. Laughs owner Phil Scotti, most customers complained "You didn't do anything. What took you so long?" The interior was thoroughly cleaned, but not de-patinized or depersonalized. The exterior was left intact but received a much-needed shoring up. Just to make sure the bar's original character was preserved, though, the old gang came out to the reopening. The lines were out the door and four deep at the bar. The regulars were here and they wanted their bar back. They got it back, and in even better shape than before.

The fierce loyalty the patrons of P. J. Clarke's show has a lot to do with the bar's history. Founded in 1884, by 1902 it was being run by an Irishman named Duneen. It was Duneen who hired Patrick J. Clarke. Clarke eventually bought the saloon 1912 and renamed it. The Clarke family ran the place until 1948, when the Lavezzo family, local antique dealers and restorers, bought it. They also bought the building, a fateful purchase, on the eve of the skyscraper boom of the fifties, and the demolition of the Third Avenue El (elevated subway).

The minute the El came down, the whole place changed. Real estate prices took off, as Midtown moved East. Everyone sold off and moved out, to make way. The Lavezzos hung on. During that period P.J. Clarke's looked an awful lot like the little house in Virginia Lee Burton's childhood classic of the same name. The tiny old building was left behind as the huge skyscrapers went up, one by one. By 1967, the Lavezzos negotiated an agreement with a developer that allowed them to keep running P.J. Clarke's on a 99-year lease. A developer built an office complex around it. A lesser joint would have been lost, swallowed up by such an overwhelming setting.

*The developer built an office complex around it. A lesser joint would have been lost, swallowed up by such an overwhelming setting.*

But Clarke's managed to stay, serving the construction workers and the local office crowd. And the new neighborhood grew to love the old place. It was quaint, it was charming—like stepping back in time. High ceilings, carved wood, the mahogany bar built by Ehret's. The old fashioned stained glass, even in the men's restroom above the urinals. These urinals, by the way, are the most famous in all New York. Huge and made of marble, in the old days they were filled with blocks of ice, but alas, the flooding ruined the floors over the years and that tradition was stopped. Sinatra was among their biggest fans. "Those urinals!" he reportedly said. "You could stand [New York Mayor] Abe Beame in one of them and have room to spare."

The urinals aren't the only beloved feature. The place is full of quirks. There are human leg bones, crossed on the rafters, supposedly an Irish good luck charm. There are the ashes of a former regular, Phillip Kennedy, kept behind the bar. (His daughter attended the reopening, holding the urn throughout the evening.) There's the stuffed dog, Jessie, a former bar mascot that met an untimely death under a car on Third Avenue. The regulars took up a collection to get her a round trip ticket to the taxidermist's. And the pricing structure was odd, with stuff selling for $2.90 or $4.10, rather than rounded off to the nearest 50 cents, as most places do. (Today the fish and chips is $15.15.) Customers had to write up their own orders, too. Last but not least, there's the Wives' Window, the so-called beer window that served women (who weren't allowed in until the sixties) and kids who came by in the old days to get dad's dinner pail of beer. The beer window came in handy during Prohibition as well, for isn't there an old saying that when a door closes, a window opens? It's no wonder that by the 1950s Clarke's had become an institution.

AUCHENTOSHEN "TRIPLE"
BRUICHLADDICH 10 YEAR
OBAN 14
BALVENIE 21
BUNNAHABHAIN 12
DALWHINIE 15 YEAR
GLENFIDDICH 12 YEAR
GLENLIVET 12 YEAR
GLENMORANGIE 10 YEAR
GLENFARCLAS 12 YEAR
LAPHROAIG 10 YEAR
MACALLAN 12 YEAR
MACALLAN 18 YEAR
CRAGGANMORE 12 YEAR
TALISKER 10 YEAR
LAGAVULIN 16 YEAR
SINGLE MALTS
Beers On Tap
GUINNESS
SMITHWICK'S
Leffe Blonde
Boddingtons
Sam Adams
Stella Artois
Bass Ale
Grolsch
WINES BY THE GLASS
ARTICHOKE DIP
PIGS IN BLANKET

The Lavezzos didn't mind. They had Johnny Mercer sitting at the bar writing "One for My Baby," and Nat King Cole declaring the cheeseburges to be "The Cadillac of Burgers." Buddy Holly proposed to his wife (no, not Peggy Sue) after bringing her by limo to P.J. Clarke's. Frank Sinatra and Liz Taylor loved to sneak in late and hang out, and when Richard Harris was in the house, he never had to place his order for double vodkas—they just kept them coming.

*Buddy Holly proposed to his wife (no, not Peggy Sue) after bringing her by limo to P.J. Clarke's.*

Jackie and Ari's favorite table was No. 20. Charles Jackson, writer of the famous boozer movie *The Lost Weekend* was a regular, and Ray Milland shot his bar scenes from that film here. Joan Crawford, married to Pepsi Chairman Alfred Steele, came in one day to return his P. J. Clarke's credit card after he passed away. It's still framed, behind the bar.

Stars still come to Clarke's and to the upstairs room called Sidecar. Clubby, white tableclothed, beautifully lit, this place with its oyster bar and filet mignon is an updated Victorian dining room. A quiet elegance permeates the place, and the service is impeccable. There are no stuffed dogs or crossed bones here, and the only ashes you might see are from fine Cuban cigars. Sidecar is the other secret to P. J. Clarke's reclaimed popularity. Not advertised except by "word of mouth," the reservations-only dining room is as packed for lunch and dinner as the downstairs bar. Only it's much, much quieter. Here is where Brooke Shields had her baby shower and where Johnny Depp gave Keith Richards a guitar. (Richards immediately tested it out by serenading the room with a version of "Brown Sugar.") Cuba Gooding, Jr., Ashley Judd, Matt Dillon, Renée Zellweger, Don Mattingly, Warren Beatty, and even Gen. Tommy Franks have enjoyed this annex to P. J. Clarke's.

And so, the renovation worked and the bar remains a New York institution for another century to come.

DRINKING
ALCOHOLIC BEVERAGES
DURING PREGNANCY
CAN CAUSE
BIRTH DEFECTS
BOTTLED BEER
AMSTEL LIGHT
BECKS
BUDWEISER
COORS LIGHT
CORONA
CORONA LIGHT
HEINEKEN
KILLIAN'S RED
Kitchen Open
Nightly
GOVERNMENT
WARNING:
P.J. Clarke's Hamburgers
Baked Artichoke Dip
Pigs in a Blanket
Park Avenue Steak Tartare
Bar Hangar Steak & Fries
Raw Bar Sampler
The Clarke's Sampler
Budweiser

48
Spring Lounge
Spring Lounge
YOU MUST BE 21 YEARS OLD TO ENTER THE BAR

# Spring Lounge

48 Spring Street

AMSTEL
light
PALE ALE
BROOKLYN
BROOKLYN IPA
Hoegaarden
The Original Belgian White Beer
Hoegaarden
Since 1445
YUENGLING
TRADITIONAL
LAGER
SPRING LOUNGE
ALE
Schaefer
BEER
STELLA ARTOIS

*When owners Bryan Delaney and Dave Broderick took over the Spring Lounge, formerly the Shark Bar, regulars and locals looked on with suspicion.*

Was their beloved dive going to become gentrified? It seemed so likely an outcome that a funeral was held on the last night Pat Cacerta owned it. Folks were so sure that the place would never be the same, they walked off with most of the bar's famous stuffed sharks, which had been caught by Cacerta and her husband, Jimmy "Red" Cacerta. Bryan Delaney laughs, remembering the sight of regulars tottering down the street after the funeral, "a lot of them carrying sharks under their arms."

He didn't laugh at the sign over the bar that read "R.I.P. The Spring Lounge." "They were really worried we'd change the place," he says. "But we wanted to keep it a neighborhood bar." Well, yes, but within reason. After all, the neighborhood, like the bar, was seedy. There was Eddie the bartender, always working in a dirty T-shirt (dirty meaning soiled as well as obscene). There were the customers, too, mostly men, some of them from Bowery hotels (in fact, a few of the barkeeps lived at the Sunshine Hotel.) There were the signs that advertised beer that wasn't even sold at the bar. There were dogs that wandered in off the street. The tables and chairs, like the customers and staff, were old and worn, with cracked surfaces. The regulars adored their glorious dump and didn't want it changed one bit. But Delaney observed that there were plenty of potential customers in the neighborhood who weren't so enamored with this well-known old man's bar. "Women would walk by and sorta look in the window and keep going," he says.

*The regulars adored their glorious dump and didn't want it changed one bit.*

He sought to change that, but he knew from experience it would be slow work. It had already taken a year of protracted, difficult negotiations with Cacerta to buy the business. (Initially she'd wanted to be paid $100,000 in cash, in a paper bag.) And then the regulars began fretting that the two new owners would change the place. During this time, the poor Spring Lounge sat there, burdened by its crazy but loveable family. Fortunately Delaney and Broderick were not squeamish. They knew the bar was worth it and were willing to put up with a lot to get it. They hung in there, finally getting the bar and making small changes over time. With a history tenaciously clung to in the neighborhood, it was not easy.

Shark Bar started out as a bucket-of-beer shop during Prohibition, then it was Chappy's in the 1940s, and Wilson's 10:30 in the 1960s (named after the time of the nightly craps game). When Pat Cacerta bought the place she named it after the sharks she and her husband love to catch, but she may have been naming it after her husband and his friends. Red Cacerta was a tough guy who loved a good time. Unfortunately his good times ended when he was found dead on Staten Island, possibly killed in retaliation for a murder he had committed. After running the place for 20 years, Pat decided to sell the bar and pizza parlor.

*Red Cacerta was a tough guy who loved a good time. Unfortunately his good times ended when he was found dead on Staten Island, possibly killed in retaliation for a murder he had committed.*

Delaney and Broderick began by incorporating the old with the new. Eddie stayed on a while as bartender, and the regulars felt welcome. The old chairs and tables stayed until Delaney and Broderick built replacement tables from wood found in the basement, one of the last dirt basements left in New York City. (The table legs were made in Williamsburg, Brooklyn, from logs used to support cranes during construction.) The drop ceiling was taken down (a tin ceiling discovered underneath), brick walls were uncovered, and the pizza parlor next door was annexed, almost doubling the bar's size. But most of it was left "as was." Delaney even hired a regular and bartender from some years back, Joe Vaccaro.

Like a lot of Bowery men, Joe had a past shrouded in some mystery, but was basically a good soul, in need of a job. Delaney gave him one as day bartender (they opened at 8 a.m.), and for the first few days, all went well. Joe was reliable, and he knew the customers. He lived around the corner at the Sunshine. Then on the fifth day, Delaney was expecting a delivery and gave Vaccaro an envelope containing $650 cash to pay for the goods. There was something about that envelope that set Joe off. He told a customer, "I'm going to get lemons," and he never came back. Delaney still shakes his head, remembering. "He didn't take money from the register or the safe, just that envelope. And he disappeared." Locals were shocked at the suddenness of Joe's departure. "He'd been in the neighborhood for twenty-three years, so everyone around here couldn't believe it. They said to me 'What'd ya do to him?'" sighs Delaney. As for old Joe, he's never showed his face at the Spring Lounge or in the neighborhood again.

One good thing happened the day Joe Vaccaro walked. Jay Hammer jumped behind the bar and hasn't left since.

Jay Hammer is an investor in this bar and several others in the city. He happened to be here when Joe took off, and he started manning the bar when it became obvious that those lemons weren't going to show up any time soon. Hammer, an actor who starred as Fletcher Reade on *Guiding Light*, is a natural fit behind the bar. Between the fans and the regulars who come for his shift, it's a good match for the Spring Lounge and Hammer.

Since those early days in 1996, the neighborhood has changed quite a bit, the bar changing with it. The street crime is way down. There's a younger crowd and a younger staff. Twelve taps featuring boutique beers and ales. (Delaney used to be a beer salesman for the Brooklyn Brewery.) The bar seems to have found a comfortable niche carved from its history and the neighborhood. Finally, the Spring Lounge can rest a bit, in peace.

THE
WHITE HORSE
Eſtab. 1742

# White Horse Tavern

567 Hudson Street
at 11th Street

White Horse
TAVERN
RYE
SCOTCH
LIQUEURS

*You can drink in history and a crisp ale or two at the White Horse Tavern. Originally built in 1817 as a bookstore, the White Horse sits on a historic parcel of land.*

Once part of Sir Peter Warren's estate, it was given to his son-in-law, Lord Abingdon, who sold it in 1815 to the Sewell family. (The property remained in the hands of the Sewells until 15 years ago.) The Tavern's pedigree is extensive. It reaches back to the mid-nineteenth century when it was known as the James Dean Oyster Bar and stretches to 1880, when it became the White Horse. Step into that wood frame building, one of the few left in the City, and you're stepping into old New York, when the West Village was peopled by the men who worked the Hudson River docks, and the families they struggled to raise.

The West Village was a close-knit neighborhood, home to many Irish immigrants whose children grew up to become the backbone of New York life and politics, from the fire and police departments to city administration. In this neck of town, the business of bar-running was more elastic than in other parts of the City; rules were bent, or totally ignored, as during Prohibition, when the White Horse operated openly. It was never closed and never raided, and it never even pretended to be anything but the White Horse Tavern. Of course, it didn't hurt that Mayor Jimmy Walker had grown up five blocks away (his father having built many houses along Hudson Street), or that the White Horse was Hizzoner's favorite watering hole. Dapper and dandy though he was, Walker remained a neighborhood boy, drinking with the working class men he'd known all his life.

A longshoreman's and truck driver's bar it was and remained, until the mid 1950s, when the White Horse began to attract political activists, artists, musicians, and writers, most famous among them Dylan Thomas. The White Horse reminded him of pubs back home in Wales, and Thomas settled in as a regular, to drink and carouse, loudly, lustily, and notoriously. Crowds assembled just to see him in action. And so it was on a November night in 1953, just after his thirty-ninth birthday, that Thomas went, not "gentle into

that good night," but hard, falling like a stone, after a bout of heavy drinking. "That's my eighteenth whiskey; I think that's a record," were his last words, spoken to the White Horse crowd. They carried him to St. Vincent's Hospital around the corner, where he died days later, never regaining consciousness. His death shocked the literary world and made the White Horse famous. Says Ed Brennan, current owner (and a regular himself during Thomas's era), "To this day every English major in the tri-state area comes into the White Horse to see where Dylan Thomas used to hang out and where he died."

The White Horse continues to be a pilgrimage stop for artistic types, for not only Thomas drank there, but also Jack Kerouac. (Kerouac was barred frequently, and once wrote that someone had written "go home Kerouac" on the men's room wall.) Norman Mailer, James Baldwin, Delmore Schwartz, Anais Nin, Pete Hamill, and Jimmy Breslin. Bob Dylan used to drop in to watch the Clancy Brothers perform. Actors John Belushi, Dan Aykroyd, Jessica Lange, Demi Moore, Bill Hickey, Robert De Niro, and former mayors Robert Wagner, Ed Koch, and David Dinkins were among the notables who frequented the place.

Brennan is protective of his famous regulars, which is probably why they continue to come. He let the Lovin' Spoonful crash at his upstairs apartment when they needed to sleep it off, and he would sit and chat with John Kennedy, Jr. when he was a frequent lunch customer in his law school days. The wildest partier of them all? Belushi, of course. A nice guy and a great tipper, he was a favorite of the waitresses, but Brennan adds "I'd have to keep my eye on him all the time, I was so afraid he was going to hurt himself." When in town, Dan Aykroyd would call, and Brennan would close the bar at 2 a.m. Whoever was there was invited to stay as Aykroyd's guest, and he'd come in with a couple dozen friends or more, to party 'til 4. It's these little accommodations that make the White Horse a neighborhood bar for the rich and famous. After parties like the one for the wrap of *Sex and the City*, are not uncommon.

The White Horse inspires a loyal following among its regular customers of the nonfamous variety, too. Whether he is inviting people to sleep over during the 1965 Blackout, or assisting rescuers throughout the weeks following the 9/11 terrorist attacks (the White Horse lost two bouncers, both firefighters), Brennan has run the place with his personal touch, leading to a core of devoted regulars. (One day when fire extinguishers went off during a busy lunch, filling the bar with fine powder, the crowd stayed to help clean.) As it passes its 125th anniversary, the White Horse is in the homestretch and just got its second wind.

*Brennan has run the place with his personal touch, leading to a core of devoted regulars.*

# Index

## Bars

# People

**G**



**H**



**J**



**K**



**L**



**M**



**N**